Gun Sanity

How Societies Reduce Gun Violence

By Michael M. Nunes

I dedicate this book to all the people who have lost their lives to

gun violence, because we are unable and unwilling to enact

sensible restrictions on firearms.

Contents

Preface

"The death toll from small arms dwarfs that of all other weapons systems - and in most years greatly exceeds the toll of the atomic bombs that devastated Hiroshima and Nagasaki. In terms of the carnage they cause, small arms indeed could well be described as 'weapons of mass destruction'." (Kofi Annan, Un Secretary-General, March 2000)[1]

I am a South African, born and bred. Like Americans, South Africans worshipped the firearm; almost every white home had firearms, and many residents hunted for recreation. As in the United States, people believed guns to be a part of their heritage, a tradition holding that all South Africans should be able to shoot. Naturally, as with so many things under apartheid, the possession of firearms was mostly restricted to whites. Firearms did not allow the white regime to maintain power; rather a whole host of factors including control of economic levers, education, freedom of speech and the press, and laws circumscribing movement enabled their control. What the gun tradition did ensure was that gun deaths remained stubbornly high.

According to the United Nations, almost 1,000 people are killed each day with firearms around the world[2]. The Global Burden of Armed Violence reports that over 740,000 people are killed either directly or indirectly from armed violence each year. Most of these deaths are during non-conflict events; 490,000 deaths occur outside war zones.

In the wake of World War II, countries participating in that conflict were left with enormous stockpiles of armaments. None of the belligerents wanted responsibility for these firearms, with the result that the American market was flooded with surplus weapons. Many of these weapons were available for sale, often for less than a dollar each. Around six million foreign weapons were brought into the U.S., adding to the domestic production of cheap handguns, which was also rising.

Most of the belligerents in WW2 introduced sensible gun controls, a move that was spectacularly successful at reducing or controlling gun deaths. Only the United States refused to comply, and in fact produces laws to increase the guns available to the public, with the resultant national disgrace of death, injury and intimidation that, as history clearly shows, accompanies weapons possession.

Few international agreements have been signed limiting the proliferation of small arms around the planet. Small arms have taken more lives since the Second World War than any other weapon system. Clearly, small arms pose a far greater immediate threat to life and to national security than nuclear arms. While nuclear armaments ultimately pose the greater threat, it is the daily toll of death and grave injury, together with assault, intimidation and oppression that are of greater immediate concern.

In the United States, assault weapons and increasingly powerful handguns are readily available to almost anyone. These weapons pose a significant risk to national security through increased urban conflict and insurrection and the increasing possibility of homegrown terrorism. The ubiquity of small arms increases tensions and exacerbates urban violence. In the event of economic shocks, people are quite likely to turn to intimidation through force of arms. The longer people are allowed to collect these weapons of mass destruction, and the more in circulation, the more difficult it will become to restrict their use. Already, Stand Your Ground laws serve to legitimize homicide by blurring the boundaries between legitimate self-defense and the gratuitous taking of life.

We implement policies to reduce deaths by all causes around the globe; AIDS, bird flu, tuberculosis, and vehicle accidents, yet we appear to be incapable of doing the same with small arms. We treat the rights of those who are not armed with contempt, expecting unarmed young men to defend themselves against well-armed and more mature men. Increasingly, those who are armed have rights, while those who do not are accused of trying to seize the weapons of those who are.

In comparison to most developed nations around the world, the United States is alone in its indifference to human life in relation to gun rights. Gun owners are seen as having rights that supersede the lives of other residents of the U.S. A putative right arrogated by the gun lobby is permitted to remain extant with total disregard for the rights of peaceful non-gun-owners. Despite the dramatic successes in developed nations in reducing gun violence by restricting access to guns, the U.S. still clings to its firearms without thought for the consequences.

The NRA, instead of using scientific data to justify its extreme stance on firearms, prefers instead to attack data and science that does not accord with its beliefs, an intellectually unscrupulous way to justify their ideology. We are all subject to the dictates of verifiable data, regardless of our ideological perspective. The NRA does not get the right to dismiss verified data with which it disagrees.

Introduction

This book will argue that gun control has been successful in every country that has tried it. Every American state that has some gun restrictions has managed to keep gun deaths lower than those states without such controls. Each argument marshaled by the gun lobby against gun restrictions is then refuted by appeal to the available facts, rather than to emotion.

The gun lobby's most powerful assertion against gun restriction is that self-defense is the primary motivation for possession of firearms, even extreme weapons like assault rifles. As presented in this book, the arguments in favor of self-defense are weak, and empirical evidence in support of self-defense uses for firearms is in short supply. If the use of self-defense is extremely rare, the central argument of the gun lobby vanishes and the way is open for comprehensive gun restrictions. Even if the need for self-defense were common, the absence of firearms would negate the need for firearm possession, as is seen in most developed nations.

Around the world, almost 1,000 people die by gun each day[1], more than a third of a million people each year. The U.S. accounts for almost 10% of that total, with a population amounting to less than 5% of the global total. There are war zones that have fewer deaths.

An article in the Guardian newspaper questions whether it is time for an international intervention in the United States. The author asks whether what is happening in the United States should be viewed as a humanitarian crisis[2]. The U.S. has the tendency to interfere in every civil conflict across the globe, decrying the deaths and injuries of children, and yet similar events occur in the U.S. each day. The U.S. expresses outrage at the suffering in other countries, and yet shows itself incapable of managing its own humanitarian disaster.

In the wake of 9/11, the U.S. introduced the most draconian anti-terrorism laws in its history in the form of the PATRIOT Act, ostensibly to combat an extremely low probability event, and yet it is incapable of implementing anything similar concerning its uncontrollable gun violence. A great many more people die from gun violence in the United States than from terrorism, and yet trillions of dollars are spent fighting an almost non-existent threat of terror attacks. Nations with relatively high death rates from terror attacks are routinely given travel advisories by U.S. authorities, despite the incessant drumbeat of gun deaths in the U.S. This has little impact on lawmakers, or the public, both of whom appear oblivious to the disaster on their own doorstep.

This book confronts as many of the arguments conjured up by the gun lobby as feasible, addressing them as best as possible, with the available facts. It discusses the inability of Congress to introduce substantive gun reforms as other developed, OECD countries have done. It also compares the policies of the states within these United States and the impact those policies have on death and injury, and the dramatic differences in gun violence between developed nations.

The Gun Violence Gulf Between Restrictive and Permissive States

You don't spread democracy with a barrel of a gun **(Helen Thomas)**

While gun violence is significantly higher in the United States than it is in other developed nations, there is a diversity of outcome between the various geographic sectors of the United States, and between states. The reasons are not surprising and are easy to discern even without much available data. Since the various states have sometimes dramatically different firearm laws, it is not too complex to compare the laws of the states and the firearm death rates to determine whether there are any common threads producing similar outcomes.

The Most Dangerous States: Those with Few Gun Restrictions

A study by the Center for American Progress finds that the more legislation a state has restricting firearms, the fewer gun deaths it experiences. Those states with the weakest gun laws experience higher rates of gun homicide and suicide, deaths of children and law enforcement officers[1], which strongly suggests that gun restriction works across the states. Another recent study comparing firearm legislation across all the states finds that states in the highest quartile of legislative strength, i.e. those with the strongest gun regulations had a lower overall rate of firearm fatality than those in the lowest quartile, those with the weakest legislation[2]. States with few gun laws have gun ownership rates of up to 70% while those with the most laws have rates around 20%.

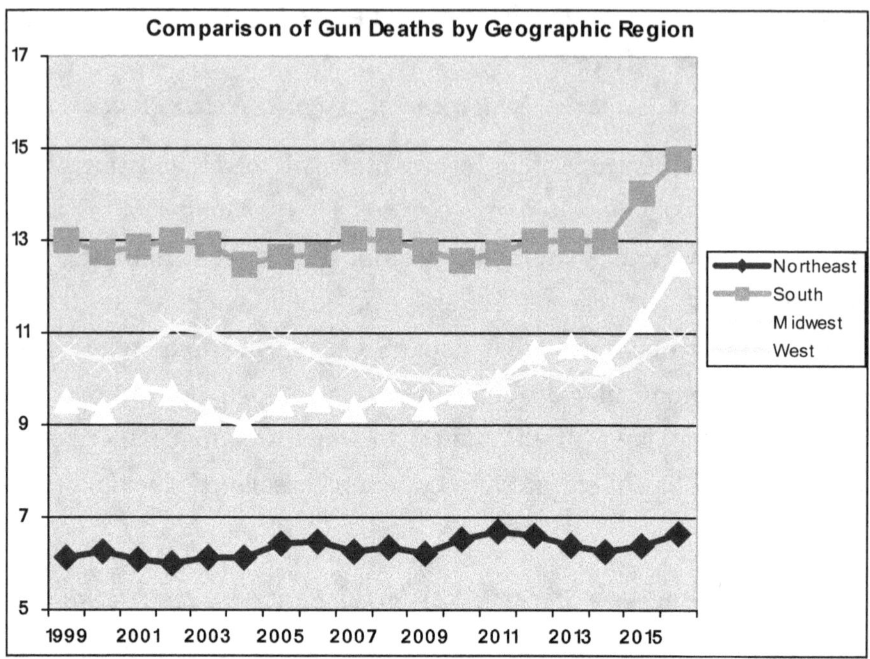

Figure 1 Comparison of Firearm Deaths Between Regions

This research shows that those states with the strictest anti-gun-violence laws are also those with the lowest gun death rates in the nation. Of the ten states with the most restrictive gun laws, seven have the lowest gun death rate. At the same time, those states with the most relaxed gun laws have the highest death rate by gun. If border controls were in place to prevent guns flooding into states with gun regulation from states without controls, the death rate would likely fall even farther. The pro-gun states are thus at least partly accountable for many of the firearm deaths and injuries in those states with stricter gun legislation.

States with low gun death rates are in the forefront of introducing more stringent anti-gun-violence laws, demonstrating their willingness to protect their citizens, in sharp contrast to those states with high gun death rates. Subsequent to the Newtown shootings, New York State passed a ban on assault weapons and large capacity magazines, while Illinois moved forward with a similar ban. Both New Jersey and Connecticut are considering such bans, albeit at a more measured pace, appointing task forces to study the issue.

Gun regulation laws vary widely between the various states, with some legislation governing at the federal level, but much left to the states to decide. A recent study ranked the states on a point system, which added points for background checks, assault weapons and high-capacity magazine bans, and concealed weapons permits. Points were lost for legal immunity extended to gun sellers and bans on doctors providing information to patients on firearm risk.

The states with the weakest laws lined up with the rates of violence and trafficking; South Dakota, Arizona, Mississippi, Vermont, and Louisiana. Those states with the strongest anti-gun-violence laws were California, New Jersey, Massachusetts, Connecticut and Hawaii. With the exception of Vermont, all the states with the weakest anti-gun-violence laws were Southern and Mountain West, while all the strongest states were Pacific or Northeastern[3]. The 10 states with the weakest gun laws have a gun violence rate more than twice that in the states with the strongest gun laws.

A number of factors may influence gun violence rates, including crime patterns and various socio-economic issues including poverty rates, and educational levels. It is difficult to determine whether people buy guns to protect themselves from high crime rates, or whether gun possession causes high crime rates. It may well be that they reinforce one another in a vicious cycle of violence. If that is true, it is still better to reduce the guns available, which over time should reduce the crime rate. However, having said that, the higher the number of positive correlates, the more likely it is that we can infer causation.

David Kopel, assistant policy analyst at the Cato Institute says that Louisiana is a low control state with a lot of crime, which explains its position as the state with the highest firearm murder rate in the nation. However, he says that New York and California are dangerous states in comparison with the rest of the country and they are high control states[4]. This is clearly incorrect based on the evidence, as I will show.

States with Few Gun Laws and More Guns Experience Higher Crime and Violence

According to Uniform Crime Reporting Statistics data, the rate of violent crime in New York State is below the national average of 403, while California is very slightly above[5]. Louisiana, on the other hand, is substantially above the average as are Alaska and Arkansas, both states with few controls on firearms[6]. Hawaii has the lowest gun crime rate of all states at 262 per 100,000.

In terms of violence, states like Arkansas, Missouri, New Mexico, and South Carolina, all have violent crime rates that exceed those in New York State and the national average[7]. Similarly, their gun death rate is higher than in New York State.

In comparison with cities of over one million residents, New York City[8] has one of the lowest crime rates in the U.S., a little more than the entire state of Louisiana. Crime rates in highly urbanized areas tend to be higher than in rural or smaller cities due to the higher concentration of people. In comparison, in a state with lenient gun restriction laws, Houston, Texas[9] has a crime rate almost double that of New York City. New York City has one of the lowest gun death rates for cities in the nation at 4.9 per 100,000 compared with cities like Las Vegas (36.9) and New Orleans (69.1). Contrary to the claim by David Kopel, New York City is one of the safest cities in which to live in the United States. There appears to be a correlation between the levels of gun ownership and higher crime. It may have something to do with poverty, educational levels and level of state involvement, but those are all issues easily addressed by the state.

The same ideology that places the burden for poverty, education and public infrastructure on the individual instead of on the state where it belongs also increases violence and the rate of gun deaths. Thus, it is the state political philosophy and the culture of selfishness, which includes fewer gun laws and allows more guns, that is in no small part responsible for higher gun deaths.

The U.S. Peace Index (USPI) is a statistical way of ranking states according to their level of peacefulness. Developed by the Institute for Economics and Peace, it ranks states on five primary indicators; homicides, violent crimes, incarceration, police officers and the availability of small arms all measured per 100,000 people. Conservatives like David Kopel of the Cato Institute claim that the Northeast is more violent than the rest of the country, but this does not accord with the facts. The Northeast, according to the USPI, is the most peaceful region of the country, with the lowest rates of homicide, violent crime and incarceration. The South, predictably, is the least peaceful, with the highest rates of homicide, violent crime and incarceration[10]. There are some exceptions to these statistics. Maryland, really a border state between North and South, has a high rate of crime, probably due to Baltimore, which has high rates of poverty, economic disparities and racial segregation.

The conservative claim that higher levels of gun ownership will lower violent crime rates similarly does not accord with the facts. If this were in fact the case, the Southern states would be the most peaceful in the nation, with the lowest rate of violent crime, all else being equal. That they are not partially highlights the failure of gun ownership to lower violent crime. Despite the ever increasing number of guns sold in the country, particularly in the Southern states, (over 300 million guns nationally, or one per person) violent crime, gun homicide and suicide remains higher in those states with more guns and lower in those with fewer guns. Some of these states have violent crime rates on a par with the most violent nations on Earth.

It may well be that since Southern states have such a high rate of gun ownership people feel that their only defense is to arm themselves. Similarly, in poverty stricken inner cities with high crime rates, the residents may feel it necessary to arm themselves because so many of their neighbors are armed. Students in poorer areas may feel that they need arms to protect themselves while traveling to and from school. The most rational solution is to remove firearms and people will no longer feel the need to carry firearms. This may well be the reason the Northeastern states are able to institute gun restrictions so easily in comparison to southern states; since there are fewer guns, people do not feel the need to protect themselves.

The economic policies of Southern States are largely to blame for higher rates of violence. Lackluster public spending and investment in education leads to unemployment and increased poverty, which produces more violence. Negligent gun laws allow violence to become fatal more quickly, which aggravates the social malaise. This leads more people to procure firearms for personal protection, leading to more gun death. The Southern states thus produce their own dilemma with increased firearm availability and lower investment in their citizens.

Negligent Gun Laws Encourage Interstate Trafficking from Unregulated States to Restrictive States

A 1996 study in Virginia found that the proportion of crimes committed in the Northeast with firearms traced to dealers in Virginia declined by 30% subsequent to the implementation of the one-gun-per-month law in that state[11]. The group Pennsylvania Against Trafficking Handguns claims that Virginia's share of guns recovered in the Northeast fell by 54% after the introduction of the law.

Virginian officials concluded, "*The statute has had its intended effect of reducing Virginia's status as a source state for gun trafficking*"[12]. Such laws are demonstrably effective at preventing the illegal interstate transfer of firearms. In 2013, Virginia repealed the law despite its demonstrated success in reducing gun trafficking.

Thus, the careless gun laws in one state can have a profound influence on crime in other states. It is for this reason that states' gun restrictions in the U.S. may fail in their primary objective of reducing gun crime, placing the onus for much gun crime on those states without gun restrictions. This is certainly one explanation for the high firearm death rate in Washington D.C. and Chicago, both of which have strict gun laws and relatively high levels of gun violence; many of those firearms are brought in from surrounding states with weak laws.

Despite the ease with which firearms are obtained at gun shows in particular, the Virginia State Legislature has twice refused to close this loophole. Gun rights advocates claim that it would be bad for business at gun shows and violate privacy rights. Some research shows that gun shows account for significant increases in gun crime; society should have the right to its security, which should trump any right to profits lost by gun sellers. Gun sellers and show organizers fear that that background checks would hurt sales, but that is the point; to stop people prohibited from gun possession from obtaining them freely through the gun show system.

Mississippi exported more than 50 guns per 100,000 residents to other states, many of which were subsequently used in violent crimes in those states. While the gun homicide rate in Mississippi is 6.91, the second highest in the nation, it also increases the rate of crime by exporting its guns to other states.

The gun policies of Southern and Mountain West states are dangerous to their own citizens; they are also more dangerous to the citizens of other states. The export rate of crime gun measures how many guns sold in one state are recovered in crimes in other states. According to the Center for American Progress,

> "The top 10 states for the export of these crime guns had a rate of export to other states almost double the national average and more than three times those states with the lowest export rates"[13].

Based on the recovery of crime guns, these ten states supplied 49% of guns that crossed state lines before being recovered in crimes. This accounts for 21,000 crime guns recovered in 2009. These states are all Southern states with weak anti-gun-violence laws. Those top ten states accounted for almost half of the crime guns crossing state lines, exporting crime guns at a rate seven times that of the ten states with the lowest export rates. Rounding out the top states are Mississippi, West Virginia, Alaska, Alabama, South Carolina, Virginia, Indiana, Nevada, Georgia, and Kentucky. At the bottom were the usual states with the highest level of gun restriction, Hawaii, New York, New Jersey, Massachusetts and California[14]. Far too many people die or are injured in other states due to the capricious and careless gun laws in Southern states.

ATF trace data show *"substantial interstate smuggling of handguns"* according to the National Economic Research Associates (NERA). This smuggling is inevitably from states with few gun restrictions to those with more controls. According to the ATF,

> "In 2006, 71% of New York State's and 66% of Massachusetts's crime guns originated out of state"[15].

There is a high markup on cheap guns; a $99 firearm in Georgia could fetch $600 in New York City according to a study by Mayors Against Illegal Guns[16].

Another measure of gun crime is the time between a firearm sold in a state and the time it is used in a crime. This is a measure of the relationship between licensed retailers and gun trafficking networks. The ATF considers a time to crime of less than two years a strong indication of illegal trafficking. The states with the most trafficking, Missouri, Arizona, Alaska and Louisiana were no surprise, but New Hampshire was surprising, exporting many of its guns into the New York/New Jersey metropolitan area. The states with the lowest time to crime were Hawaii, Massachusetts and New Jersey[17].

States with negligent gun laws have a dramatic impact on the states and cities around them. Washington D.C introduced strict gun laws in 1976, and Chicago in 1982, yet gun crime, and suicide, a proxy for gun availability, continued at high levels. Guns continue to flow into the two cities because of the lack of significant gun restrictions in the surrounding states. Gun proponents point to both cities as examples of failed gun regulations without understanding the trafficking of firearms into the cities from other sources.

A border fence surrounds neither city, nor do they have import controls or immigration officers to monitor the flow of arms into each city. It is unrealistic in a nation overflowing with firearms that controls in one state or city will entirely override the flood of firearms in surrounding states. The fault lies almost entirely with those states that do not implement adequate controls on the availability of firearms.

If we were to implement controls in buffer states around Chicago and Washington D.C., it is more feasible that controls would work as intended. This can be seen in New York City, which has comparatively rigorous controls on firearms, as do the states surrounding the City; New Jersey, Connecticut, Massachusetts and New York State. Firearm death rates in New York City are among the lowest of all large cities in the nation, despite wealth disparities and a nation overflowing with firearms. This demonstrates that gun restriction works when implemented judiciously.

States with high rates of crimes caused by imported guns ought to take legal action against those states with lax gun laws to recover the costs incurred by gun violence. The citizens of one state should not have to withstand the worst of ill-considered laws in other states. If it were possible to do, states with strict gun regulation should close their borders to other states, or at least inspect vehicles for firearms at their borders.

States with High Gun Ownership Rates Have High Death Rates

A comparison of gun ownership rates to gun death rates between the states is quite illuminating[18]. The states with the highest gun ownership rates, Wyoming, Alaska, Montana, South Dakota, West Virginia and Mississippi also have the highest death rates by gun[19]. The average rate of ownership in those states is 57%, while the death rate is 15.5. In states with the lowest rate of gun ownership, Hawaii, New Jersey, Massachusetts, Rhode Island, Connecticut, New York, the gun death rate is also low[20]. The average rate of ownership is 13%, while the death rate is 4.2. The only state with high ownership and a lower death rate is South Dakota, slightly below the U.S. average gun death rate of 11.5, but still far higher than the average in the Northeast.

Those states with the highest rate of gun ownership, namely those states in the Deep South and Mountain West have higher rates of violent death by firearm than the national average. The highest rate is in Alaska, while the lowest is in Hawaii. Arkansas, Tennessee, Mississippi, Alabama, Louisiana, Nevada, Wyoming and Montana have the highest gun death rates in the country[21]. All of these states have indifferent firearm rules and very little gun regulation, and it shows in the incessant toll of death in those areas.

The states with the most anti-gun-violence laws have a 42% lower gun death rate than states with the fewest laws. The Northeastern states like New York and Massachusetts have the lowest rates of violent death in the nation behind Hawaii. Gun violence is higher in Republican states that tend to vote for greater access to guns and lower in those states with better gun restriction laws, usually Democratic states in the Northeast and Pacific.

Another study of the 50 states found similar results using 10 indicators of gun violence including overall firearm deaths in 2010, firearm deaths from 2001 through 2010, and overall homicides with firearms, among women, children and law enforcement. The states with the highest ranking of gun violence are the same Southern states as in the previous study, Louisiana, Alaska, Alabama, Arizona, and Mississippi. The states with the lowest ranking of gun violence were Hawaii, Massachusetts, Connecticut, New Jersey, and New York with only two standouts from the Midwest, Iowa and Nebraska[22].

The highest rate of homicide and suicidal gun death correlates positively with those states that voted for John McCain in 2008, in other words, those who voted Republican. This implies that states voting Republican are more likely to have incautious firearm laws and higher rates of death and injury by firearm. The next most important indicator is the level of poverty, or the number of working class residents in an area. Having weapons in high schools is next highest, leading the lie to the concept of having more guns making people safer. More guns in schools leads inexorably to more gun deaths[23]. No correlation was found between gun deaths and stress, mental illness or neuroses, despite the heavy emphasis on mental illness evinced by the pro-gun lobby.

Republican policies increase the levels of poverty, and the availability of firearms in states under their control, and ensure lower educational standards, all of which lead to increased violence and a greater number of gun deaths and injuries. By implication, voting Republican raises the life risk of living in those states. Irresponsible social policies are thus directly responsible for the dramatically higher gun death rates in Republican controlled states.

There is a negative correlation with gun violence for college graduates, those who voted Obama, voted Democratic, or were creative people, all of which shows that those with a more liberal mindset are less likely to kill one another. Another discovery was that the safe storage of firearms, bans on assault weapons, and trigger locks similarly correlates with fewer gun deaths. The Supreme Court decision forcing Washington D.C. to remove its mandate on trigger locks is thus responsible for any increase in firearm death rates in that city.

David Kopel of the Independence Institute believes that homicides are higher in some states since more people are able to defend themselves. Kopel and the gun lobby redefine self-defense, as witness the Stand Your Ground laws, to include behavior considered homicidal in most civilized nations. He presents no evidence to suggest that any of the increased killings were justifiable. It is odd that in states and nations with fewer firearms, the people do not see homicide as justifiable. Justifying homicide by redefining it as self-defense is rather like calling rape "a justifiable release of desire due to increased hormone production" without first determining whether it was a consensual act. The presence of firearms is more likely to make any violence more lethal. Manipulating data to produce a metamorphosis from homicide to self-defense cannot be seen as an ethical position.

Kopel implies that homicides are more likely to be justifiable in those states with more firearms. Laws introduced in developed nations other than the United States are mostly specific when dealing with homicide, defining what can and cannot be considered an unlawful act when taking life. Self-defense laws similarly have been well defined for centuries, circumscribing the lengths to which people may go to defend themselves. The presence of firearms in no way alters the basis by which societies judge what may be considered homicide. The very idea that the presence of a firearm somehow justifies taking a life in the name of self-defense is ludicrous.

Instances in which a person is assaulted are unlikely to end in death unless a firearm is involved. The presence of firearms only increases the risk of unnecessary death for arbitrary reasons. Self-defense should not be a license to take life as it has become in the United States. The odds against losing ones life during an assault in the absence of firearms are particularly low, and claiming that a firearm is necessary to prevent simple assault is tantamount to establishing the individual as judge, jury and executioner. Nations with well-developed laws recognize that the law must be the ultimate arbiter of disputes between individuals, whether parties have deceased or not. In the United States, appeals to the justice system are increasingly dispensable as individuals are empowered to mete out their own arbitrary justice.

It also places the individual that is not similarly armed at a distinct disadvantage over someone who is armed. Those who do not wish to arm themselves should not have to endure the risk that is attendant in any society with ubiquitous firearm ownership. The putative rights of those who are armed do not supersede the rights of people who choose not to arm themselves. This creates a society in which those who are unarmed relinquish their right to be safe and secure in their persons because so many are armed.

Cities and Metro Areas with High Gun Ownership Are More Dangerous

The same dynamic is at play in comparisons between cities or metro areas as between states or nations. The metro areas with the highest death rates are New Orleans, Birmingham and Memphis[24], an average of 24 deaths per 100,000, while those with the lowest rates are Providence, San Jose and Boston, an average of 3.8[25]. Those urban areas allowing more guns have higher death rates, while those with gun regulations have lower death rates.

In terms of cities, the highest numbers were in Detroit, Las Vegas and Miami [26]. The lowest were in San Diego, New York City and San Jose[27]. A claim by ALEC to the effect that the death rate in New York City is the highest in the country is *ipso facto* false[28]. These cities with the highest gun homicide rates are comparable to the nations with the highest rates of violence on Earth, including Guatemala, El Salvador, Columbia, Brazil and South Africa. If it were a country, New Orleans would rank as the second most violent nation on Earth, with 62.1 gun deaths per 100,000, almost on a par with Honduras at 68.4 deaths per 100,000. The safest large cities in the nation are in those states with the highest levels of gun restriction, while the least safe are in those regions with firearm anarchy.

New Orleans is a particularly dangerous city for its residents, due primarily to its non-existent gun laws, placing its most vulnerable populations at greatest risk of gun death and injury. Exacerbating this situation is the low level of academic achievement, and poverty that is the hallmark of more violent societies. Just as with states with low academic outcomes and high levels of poverty, the policies of state and local government has much to do with high levels of violence and gun death. Making guns universally available, those states are complicit in the unwarranted death and injury of their citizens. These policies have simple solutions, which include restricting access to the means of death and injury, namely the firearms, and implementing policies that ease the path for improvements in the job markets and associated improvements in wealth.

The appalling manner in which residents of New Orleans were abandoned to the vagaries of Hurricane Katrina by their state and local government, and stripped of accommodation in the aftermath of that storm is a clear demonstration of the contempt with which those authorities treat their citizens. It is no wonder that those authorities care little about the death and injury of their citizens if their disregard for the general well-being is so openly displayed.

High Ownership States Are the Most Dangerous for Women and Children

The statistics in most U.S. states are no more reassuring given the firearm homicide rate for women, which is usually lower than it is for men. The same states appearing at the higher end of the gun ownership list are the states most lethal for women, with Louisiana, Mississippi, Alabama, South Carolina and Georgia all leading the way. At the lowest end of the spectrum are Massachusetts, Hawaii, Rhode Island and New Hampshire[29].

The same Southern and Mountain West states are equally as dangerous for children, with Alaska and Louisiana way out at the higher end, followed by Montana, New Mexico and Mississippi. The safest states for children are predictably New Hampshire, Massachusetts, Connecticut and Maine. The safest states for residents, women and children are all in the Northeast, with the least safe, predictably in the South and Mountain West[30].

Of the states in which women were murdered by men with firearms in 2010, the highest rates all occurred in Southern states with few gun regulations[31]; Nevada, South Carolina, Tennessee, Louisiana, Virginia and Texas. The lowest rates were all in states with tighter gun regulation laws[32], other than South Dakota; South Dakota, Illinois, Minnesota, and New Hampshire[33]. In states requiring a background check for each handgun sale, intimate partners shoot 38% fewer women to death[34].

It is clear that more liberal states, with better infrastructure, better educational standards and higher taxes are all states that are safer for women and children. Tougher gun laws also contribute to the general well-being, an indication of the efficacy of such laws. Much tighter gun restrictions across the country demonstrate a respect for human and animal life that is absent across much of the Deep South and Mountain West. Women and children are particularly vulnerable to firearm death, injury, assault and intimidation. Given that men own most firearms, and even more often by aggressive men, women and children in those homes are at particular risk.

It is ironic that the argument in favor of gun ownership, to protect the family itself creates a far more dangerous environment for the occupants of homes with firearms. This risk is far higher than the risk of death or injury during home invasion. It is senseless to take on a higher risk to mitigate a relatively low risk of death and injury. A similar reasoning is used to justify firearms in schools, itself creating a far more dangerous environment than banning firearms entirely from school property. It appears that in order to prevent a low risk event in both the home and in school, conservatives demand the right to increase risk for all members of the community.

Gun Deaths Now Exceed Motor Vehicle Deaths in Many High Gun Ownership States

In Indiana, the number of people dying in firearm incidents now exceeds the number dying in motor vehicle accidents. There were 715 motor vehicle deaths in that state compared with 735 gun deaths. The negligent gun laws in Indiana make firearm possession more dangerous than driving a motor vehicle. This is now also the case in Alaska, Arizona, Colorado, Michigan, Nevada, Oregon, Utah, Virginia and Washington[35].

In a nation that has managed to reduce motor vehicle deaths through sensible legislation, these states are still unable to regulate firearms, and the result is that people are losing their lives. While we have made great strides in reducing accidental death by all causes, firearm deaths remain stubbornly high; a result of gun lobby intransigence and a refusal to accede to the facts.

How Poverty, Religion and Incarceration Affect Gun Violence

It is easy to see in comparisons between countries that countries mired in poverty experience higher gun violence. Western nations like France and Germany have higher levels of gun ownership than Brazil or Colombia, and yet experience lower rates of gun violence. The reasons are clear. Western Europe has lower levels of income disparity, more stable legal and political institutions and better social support than do poorer nations, especially in Africa and South America.

The same dynamic could feasibly be used in part to explain gun violence within the United States. Cities like Baltimore and New Orleans have greater income disparities than other cities, while Southern states combine that with fewer economic opportunities, deteriorating public education, less social support, political instability, and corrupt democratic institutions, most of which are associated with lower budget receipts due to irresponsible tax cuts. Add to this the replacing of social support systems with fundamentalist religious institutions and the way is open for contempt for human life and the human suffering inherent in gun ownership.

Guns and poverty do not mix, which is ironic considering that those American states with higher poverty encourage gun ownership.

Reductions in gun ownership would result in safer cities, less crime and lower rates of incarceration.

How U.S. States Handle Gun Violence

Washington D.C: Surrounded By Guns.

In the District of Columbia, the introduction of gun licensing preceded a 25% reduction in homicides using firearms, and a 23% reduction in suicides by firearm. There were no similar reductions in homicides or suicides by other methods, which might be expected if other methods of homicide or suicide were substituted for firearms[1]. No similar decline was seen in states or metropolitan areas adjacent to the District. At least 47 deaths per year were prevented by these restrictions.

Connecticut: The Peaceful State

The massacre in Newtown may have been averted at least in part, had magazines been limited in size. Legislation along these lines was proposed in Connecticut, but the gun lobby, including NRA members, successfully defeated the proposal. The bill recommended making it a felony to possess magazines with more than 10 rounds and required owners to surrender them to law enforcement or remove them from the state[2]. Twenty-six lives might have been saved had the gun lobby not interfered in the democratic process by insisting on magazines that are not warranted under any circumstances. Opponents sent over 30,000 e-mails to legislators as part of a campaign organized by the NRA to stop the bill.

In Connecticut after the massacre, a rational approach is being taken to the gun violence that took so many little lives in Sandy Hook Elementary School. A task force was launched to study gun violence, and determine how to improve school security and mitigate violence in their communities. Instead of wildly throwing legislation at the issue, they want to study the problem and its solutions. It does not mean that they will actually implement common sense gun restrictions, but they will at least go through the motions, which is more than any Southern state is doing.

Connecticut anti-gun-violence laws are among the strictest in the United States, and it shows[3]. Connecticut ranks fourth out of 50 states in the stringency of its anti-gun-violence laws. Per capita instances of gun violence are fifth lowest in the nation, demonstrating the efficacy of gun regulation legislation. The state requires background checks for any handgun transfer at gun shows; prohibits ownership and transfer of assault weapons and imposes a two-week waiting period for long gun transfers. Handgun dealers must obtain a license and purchasers must obtain an eligibility certificate. Connecticut conducts its own background checks, rather than relying on the FBI. Any firearm stolen or lost must be reported to authorities. The state also allows local authorities to regulate firearms and ammunition[4]. These are all common sense laws that do nothing to prohibit the ownership of weapons for personal protection.

Currently, Connecticut still allows large capacity magazines and does not impose microstamping of ammunition that could assist law enforcement in tracking illegal handgun sales. Nor does it regulate ammunition sales. Enacting these restrictions would likely further mitigate the rate of gun violence.

Robert Crook, from the Coalition of Connecticut Sportsmen was quick to weigh in after the Newtown shootings, saying that a restriction on magazine capacity would[5]

> "Not have made a difference. We have a lot of good gun laws on the books. You can't control people who have never done anything wrong before and then just go off the deep end".

When circumstances change, such as manufacturers introducing large capacity magazines, legislators need to decide whether they are warranted or not. If magazine size would not have made a difference, gun owners can put up with smaller magazines, since they clearly do not need larger capacities. This is not a matter of controlling people; it is setting boundaries, as any law does. If people do not understand the limits of behavior, they have little incentive to change that behavior. If reducing the size of magazines would save a single life while the shooter has to reload, then we should do it, regardless of whether some gun owners are upset or not.

Another tack tried by the gun lobby is to talk about the jobs that might be lost if gun restrictions were introduced. James Debney, CEO of Smith and Wesson wrote to Representative Gerald Fox of Connecticut that reducing magazine size would[6]

> "Drastically impact the numerous firearms companies in Connecticut and across New England"

Reducing the size of magazines would do nothing to impact jobs at all. It may even increase the number of jobs, since if large magazines were banned, the industry would have to produce a greater number of smaller magazines to replace those outlawed. Jake McGuigan of the National Shooting Sports Foundation also threatened Connecticut with the loss of gun manufacturers from the state. These were just attempts to blackmail the state with the threat of job losses, another feeble, albeit successful attempt by the gun lobby to corrupt the political process. Timorous legislators in Connecticut were suitably cowed by the threats; they dropped the proposed law banning large magazines.

California: The Sensible State

Californian legislators considered limiting ammunition sales, requiring background checks and permits for people purchasing ammunition. In 1981, California had a firearm death rate of 16.5, thirty-first worst in the nation and above the national average. California tightened its firearm laws and by 2000, the death rate was down to 9.18 or twentieth in the nation. In 2010, the state had a rate of 7.9, ninth in the nation[7]. Once more, the evidence shows that more stringent anti-gun-violence laws lead to lower firearm death rates.

In 1982, proposition 15, proposing a freeze on handgun sales, was on the California ballot. The NRA mobilized, portraying the measure as removing the right to defend the home. One advertising spot portrayed an elderly woman in her bedroom, terrified beneath the covers as her doorknob slowly turns and she receives a busy signal from 911[8]. Given the success of this campaign in overturning the proposition, the NRA has successfully used an appeal to paranoia and unwarranted fear to defeat firearm ballot initiatives in ensuing campaigns. The NRA also initiated an aggressive voter drive among the pro-gun population to defeat the measure.

In 1989 at the Cleveland Elementary School in Stockton, California, Patrick Purdy shot and killed five schoolchildren and wounded 29 others before taking his own life. Using a Type 56 assault rifle (Chinese copy of the AK-47), he fired 106 rounds in three minutes, killing and wounding mostly Cambodian and Vietnamese refugees[9]. As a result, California first defined and then banned assault weapons. Only two Republicans voted in favor of the Roos-Roberti legislation[10]. The pro-gun Sen. Ed Davis (R-Valencia) warned that these laws would lead to future controls against other guns. He said[11]

> "We will be the first state in the nation to declare war on semi-automatic weapons. This bill is a result of sentiment, emotion and panic thinking. It's not going to make anyone safe."

If there is any war, it is one declared by owners of these extreme firearms, which cause the unnecessary death of ordinary people. Republicans and the pro-gun lobby, who prefer to fight for possession of extreme firearms, did not give the victims of this massacre a single instant's consideration. These laws only passed when law enforcement agencies lent their weight to the gun regulation battle. The bill succeeded beyond its drafters wildest ambitions, as the gun death rate dropped over the next twenty years to its current low. The prognostications of doom and gloom just did not pan out, as they normally do not. California shows how successful well-thought out gun restriction laws can be.

Assault weapons are now banned in California, and recently two major public pension funds are reviewing whether to divest their holdings of manufacturers of assault weapons. CalSTRS, the State Teachers Retirement System voted to sell holdings in three gun companies including Smith & Wesson and Sturm Ruger. CalPERS, the Public Employees Retirement System also voted on whether to divest from the two companies[12].

Additionally, there is a waiting period for firearms, which was extended from handguns to shotguns and rifles after the massacre in Stockton. High capacity magazines were banned, and many groups of people can no longer possess firearms, including felons and those who pose a danger to themselves or others.

The massacre in Stockton enabled California to introduce firearm restrictions that had a dramatic impact on the gun death rate in the state, driving it down over the next ten years. In comparison, driven by an obsessive gun lobby, the tragedy in Newtown has as yet spawned no such national legislation, leaving the U.S. population vulnerable to these firearms. California is considering further measures to mitigate gun crime, including tightening the assault weapons ban, high capacity magazines, background checks and permits to buy ammunition. In comparison, the propaganda onslaught by the gun lobby has thus far ensured that the U.S. Congress has considered no similar measures after Newtown. The gun lobby is maneuvering to get California gun laws before the U.S. Supreme Court, which may further endanger the Californian people, given the court's predisposition to further increased firearm availability.

Gun rights proponents claim that the measures in California will not stop gun violence or deaths. Given the ill-considered dearth of gun laws in adjoining states, guns will continue to flow across California's borders, having an adverse impact on firearm injuries and fatalities. The new legislation will not eliminate gun injuries, but it is highly likely that it will reduce those injuries. The nihilism of lawmakers in states like Arizona continues to weigh on responsible states like California and keep death rates high, making reductions in gun violence difficult to accomplish.

Massachusetts: A Rational State

Massachusetts's lawmakers are considering tougher anti-gun-violence legislation, including requiring gun owners to buy liability insurance, and setting standards for firearm licensing[13]. In a recent meeting of lawmakers and legislative staffers, there was almost universal commitment to ending gun violence in that state. The meeting was convened because of the tragedy in nearby Sandy Hook Elementary School, Connecticut, but the intent is to end all gun violence in that state.

Massachusetts is also considering stringent rules for firearm storage. Jim Wallace, executive director of the Gun Owners Action League claims that the Laws in Massachusetts are too confusing and convoluted and need to be overhauled. He claims, without citing any compelling evidence that the laws have been an "abject failure"[14].

Massachusetts wants to restrict gun purchases to one per month and restrict "straw sales" in which people buy guns legally and resell them to people barred from gun ownership. In addition, consideration is being given to restricting those with Severe Mental Illness from gun ownership[15].

Wallace claims that lawmakers have ignored his recommendations, such as a prohibited persons list, that includes violent felons, illegal aliens and others, prohibiting them from possessing weapons. The Wallace recommendations amount to a list prohibiting people he considers "undesirable" from owning firearms, not necessarily those who pose a danger to society. This is the reason that people target those with mental illness, immigrants and other vulnerable populations.

Colorado: Torn Between Common Sense and Gun Extremism

There is some concern over a firearm bill signed in Colorado in December 2012. That bill only serves to target those with mental illness, which may have little effect on shootings and only marginalizes hundreds of thousands of people in the state with moderate to severe mental illness. The burden of proof for restricting firearm ownership for people with mental illness was lowered from "imminent threat" to "substantial probability" of threat[16].

In Colorado in March 2013, Gov. John Hickenlooper finally acceded to pressure to introduce reasonable gun regulation measures[17]. In what came as a shock to NRA militants, the governor signed the nations latest gun restriction measure into law. A struggle between gun rights groups and Hickenlooper ends, for once with the gun zealots on the losing side. The laws will ban magazines holding more than 15 rounds, mandate background checks for all firearm sales, and impose a fee on sales to pay for the background checks.

The governor signed the law hours after the killing of Department of Corrections chief, Tom Clements, outside his home. The alleged killer fired at an officer who stopped his vehicle to question him, hitting the officer three times. Officers severely wounded the killer after a high-speed chase in which the he fired at them repeatedly.

It is peculiar that some Colorado sheriffs oppose new gun legislation. Considering that one of theirs was shot, it is natural to think that they would not want people having access to firearms. Sheriff John Cooke, Weld County said that he would not enforce any new gun laws[18]. As sheriff, he is able to prioritize laws enforced within his jurisdiction. If he is unwilling to adhere to the law as enacted by an elected legislature, he should step down as sheriff, since he clearly cannot carry out the duties he is compelled to uphold. No one has requested that he violate anyone's human rights. Sheriffs from other counties have joined Cooke in flaunting the law of the state whose laws they took an oath to obey.

The debate in Colorado was at first a cordial discussion between the governor and gun rights groups, but as the wide-ranging bill passed through the Colorado State House things became more acrimonious. The NRA stopped the pretense of cooperating with the governor and launched a website, Defend Colorado[19], to mobilize opposition in Colorado to the bills, also taking out newspaper advertisements criticizing the governor. There typically was no comment from the NRA on the shooting death of the Corrections Chief.

They termed the sensible firearm control measures,

"Draconian bills that attack on [sic] your Second Amendment".

The website claims that

"Your firearms freedom could be stolen away soon if you do not act now".

These measures are part of the law in every developed nation around the globe with the exception of this one. It cannot be said of those nations that institute common sense measures that they are draconian in any way. These laws save lives, regardless of the extremist position of the gun lobby. Draconian laws are those that impose extreme firearms on peaceful people regardless of their desire for a gun free environment.

The website further states,

"The bill is so poorly written that it will make ANY MAGAZINE purchased after July 1st illegal to own due to fanatical language inserted by anti-gun extremist New York Mayor Michael Bloomberg's puppets in Denver".

We were used to seeing language of this kind from Communist regimes in Central America and Africa during the heyday of the Soviet Empire. It is not fanatical to want citizens to be safe from gun-wielding thugs, who are carrying weapons that can butcher large numbers of people. This reaction is analogous to murderers and rapists complaining about draconian laws prohibiting them from indulging their fantasies. Of course, we see similar reactions from large financial institutions that almost wrecked the world economy complaining about draconian financial regulation.

Bills proposed in the Colorado legislature will attempt to overturn the legislation. Conservative politicians refuse to countenance any provision, regardless of how inconsequential to gun owners, that would produce a safer outcome for the residents of their state. Republicans claim that limiting magazine sizes will drive jobs from the state, but do not expand on the rationale behind this threat. Gun makers who leave the state because of the law change ought to be barred from doing business in Colorado. No state should allow itself to be blackmailed by any corporation.

Colorado has suffered two of the worst gun massacres in recent memories, which should convince the gun lobby that despite massive increases in gun ownership, people are still dying by the gun. You would think that with all those guns flooding the system, there would be no massacres, murders or suicides in that state. The massacres in the theatre in Aurora in which 12 people were slaughtered and 58 injured, and the school in Columbine in which 12 students and one teacher were murdered and 21 injured, should have woken the gun lobby to the fact that increased access to guns kills children. The gun extremists have only accelerated their calls for increasingly more efficient killing machines to be available to the public.

In Colorado after the Columbine shootings, the state closed the gun show loophole, requiring background checks for all firearm transfers. The crime export rate dropped -- Colorado fell from 17th to 32nd[20].

Subsequent to the successful implementation of gun restrictions in Colorado, two legislators were recalled because of their affirmative vote and one resigned rather than face recall. Gun owners and the NRA continue to fight reasonable and sensible gun restrictions and endanger the residents of their state, regardless of the evidence against civilian firearms.

Louisiana: The Unions' Most Violent, Gun-Plagued State

Louisiana is the most violent state in the union, and New Orleans, the most violent city. Yet, despite the evidence that loose gun policy does not work, the state is pushing for even more relaxed laws. In March 2013, voters in the state approved a constitutional amendment mandating an increased standard for enacting gun regulation legislation[21]. The net result is that felons can apply to possess firearms; it is incumbent on the state to prove that a felon is a danger to the state without referring to his criminal record. A judge in one case ruled that denying convicted felons the right to possess firearms is unconstitutional.

While this same state, along with other Southern states, is busy restricting the right to vote with voter ID laws, in clear violation of the Constitution, they allow access to guns to those who have shown that they should have no right to own guns. Clearly, the presumptive right to bear arms is more important in those states than is the right to vote or the right to abortion as confirmed by the Supreme Court, or ultimately the right to life.

The NRA-backed Louisiana amendment extends gun rights over and above those in the Second Amendment, making gun possession a fundamental right[22]. Laws such as mandating the carrying of a concealed permit for 18-20 year-olds, and campus bans may be invalidated under the amendment. Similar bills are being considered in seven other states, mostly in the South. Statutes that currently forbid the carrying of firearms in churches, schools, courthouses or street parades may similarly be struck down due to this amendment.

With a constitutional amendment, the legislature may no longer make any laws prohibiting firearms without "strict scrutiny". It is my contention that this amendment will only worsen the already deplorable gun death rate in Louisiana, and makes college campuses and other sensitive areas far more dangerous for residents and visitors. It is far better for tourists that they find safer, more sensible states to visit. It is already more dangerous to visit New Orleans than some of the most violent nations on Earth. Perhaps the State Department should issue travel advisories to potential tourists.

Given that Louisiana is the state with the highest rate of gun violence, including death and injury in the nation, it is easy to suppose that they would attempt to mitigate that violence. That they have done the opposite is a clear indication of the shameless lack of responsibility shown to their citizens.

Alabama: Unsafe for Employees

Alabama now allows gun owners to keep firearms locked in their cars, regardless of what employers desire. The state is effectively taking away the freedom of employers to maintain a safe working environment for their other employees, and the right of employees to be safe from potentially violent gun owners. It also provides fertile ground for thieves.

Missouri: Blissfully Ignoring the Fact of Gun Violence

Missouri is a state that once mandated background checks for all gun purchases. In 2007, the state changed the law to allow for the private transfer of firearms without a permit. The effect was felt almost immediately. In the three years following the change, the gun murder rate rose 25% from 4.6 murders per 100,000 to 5.6 gun murders[23]. There was also an increase in the number of guns flowing to criminals. The number of guns recovered at crime scenes within two years of purchase doubled, an indication of increased gun trafficking. As with other Southern states, Missouri clearly demonstrates its contempt and apathy towards the lives of its own citizens.

How Nations Handle Gun Regulation

I live in London and I love living in a gun free environment and long may it continue **(Clive Owen)**

Gary Kleck is noted for his stringent opposition to all gun restrictions and his virulent denunciations of most research into gun violence that does not accord with his position[1]. He claims that the U.S. is different to other developed nations and thus cannot be compared to those nations when discussing gun violence. The U.S. is the standout nation among 31 nations included in a study by the CDC. In all comparisons of homicide, suicide and accidental death, the U.S. leads developed nations by large gaps. Kleck makes much of alleged cultural differences between the U.S. and other nations, without producing reasons as to why these differences might make a difference to gun violence.

Japan and Britain both have low rates of gun violence and are as far apart culturally as it is possible to get. Britain is far closer culturally to the U.S. than it is to Japan, but still manages to keep homicides very low. Australia's history parallels that of the U.S. rather than Britain, and yet it manages to keep gun violence low. Canada has one of the longest contiguous borders with the U.S. on both the lower 48 states and the Alaskan border and has a far lower homicide rate.

Cultural differences may account for some small part of national differences, but do nothing to explain the vast gun violence gulf between most developed nations and the U.S. There is little qualitative difference in the population makeup between nations of the English-speaking world; legal systems are similar and based on historical legal precedent. Living standards between developed nations are similar, as are democratic norms, banking systems, education and the free exchange of ideas. The similarities between developed nations are far greater than the differences. Gun proponents have yet to deliver a persuasive reason for the gun violence gulf between the U.S. and all other developed nations.

Socioeconomic differences explain much of the gun violence between various parts of the U.S. and between nations, but it still does not account for the differences between nations with similar living standards and the U.S.

Gun proponents have argued both that the United States is more violent than other nations, and that gun ownership causes less violence. They must decide which argument to use, since both cannot simultaneously be true. It is unlikely that the U.S. has a higher criminal population, since incarceration rates are close to ten times what they are in the United Kingdom. Given that rate, a higher percentage of criminals would surely be incarcerated in the U.S., which should reduce the mythical criminal population. Despite high incarceration rates, gun violence continues at high levels.

The U.S: The World's Most Dangerous Developed Nation

At least 10.2 people per 100,000 died by gun in the U.S. in 2007. Compare this to those nations with strict gun restrictions, such as the United Kingdom (0.25), Germany (1.1), France (3.0), Japan (0.07), and South Korea (0.13). The evidence, based on the available data, is clear that higher rates of gun regulation correlates with lower rates of death by gun. European and Far Eastern countries, which have the strictest gun laws, also have the lowest rates of death.

In the United States, gun homicide rates have remained stubbornly high and relatively constant since 1998, while in those countries that introduced firearm controls homicides have fallen or remained at consistently low levels. The absolute rate of gun deaths in the United States remains far higher than any other industrialized nation, putting the country on a par with some countries in the developing world. The lack of gun restrictions and insistence on increasing access to guns is undoubtedly the proximate cause of the number of gun deaths each year[2]. The total number of gun deaths from all causes rose between 1999 and 2011. Non-fatal firearm injuries experienced a dramatic increase from a rate of 21.7 to 25.8.

This does not necessarily mean that the United States is a more violent or crime-ridden society than other members of the community of developed nations. Comparisons between nations find that rates of robbery, sexual assault, aggravated assault, burglary, car theft and adolescent fighting are similar across the developed world[3]. There is little evidence that strict gun regulation increases violent crime, whereas relaxed gun laws in countries like the United States lead to increased numbers of gun crimes, homicides and suicides.

The examples of Israel and Switzerland are cited as countries having large numbers of guns and low shooting deaths. Firstly, the relative number of guns in Switzerland (45.7) is half that of the United States. In Israel, there are 7.3 guns per 100 people as opposed to 88.8 in the United States. Children in the U.S. are particularly badly affected by firearm deaths and injuries. In 2005, 5,285 U.S. children were killed by gunshot compared with 57 in Germany and none in Japan.

In Terms of Gun Violence, U.S. States Rank with the World's Most Violent Nations

A comparison of firearm related death rates per 100,000 between the states and various countries is illuminating. Alaska (20.28) ranks with South Africa (21.51), which is one of the most violent nations on Earth. Louisiana (19.06) is on a par with Brazil (19.03), which is also a violent nation in terms of firearm deaths. Montana (16.58) is close to Panama (17.6), Hawaii (3.31), the lowest ranks close to the Philippines (3.24), while Massachusetts (4.12) aligns with Serbia (3.9). No U.S. state can even remotely match Japan (0.06), the United

Kingdom (0.25) or Spain (0.62) all of which have strict or rigid gun restrictions, and all of which are democracies, not authoritarian states.

The U.S. Is Defying Its International Legal Obligations

The United Nations Special Rapporteur on Violence against Women, and the Special Rapporteur on Human Rights and Small Arms says, *"States which fail to adequately regulate firearms are failing to meet their obligations under international law, particularly with respect to the safety of women and children"*[4]. The United States has always held itself aloof from the norms of international law, which has resulted in far higher gun death rates than necessary. The American people ought to consider this a serious violation of human rights and take action to mitigate gun violence. Vulnerable populations, especially children are given little choice as to whether firearms are introduced into their environment.

In comparison to other developed nations, total US homicide rates are 6.9 times higher, and firearm homicide rates 19.5 times higher than those nations. For residents aged 15 to 24, the U.S. rate is 42.7 times higher than other industrialized nations, while firearm homicide rates are 22 times higher for those ages. Women are killed at a rate 11.4 times that of other developed nations. Suicide rates are 5.8 times greater than in those developed nations. Among the 23 countries included in the poll, 80% of all firearm deaths occur in the U.S., 86% of all women killed were in the U.S. and 87% of all children killed were American[5].

The United Nations Human Rights Council released a paper detailing the obligation of states to prevent human rights violations committed with small arms and light weapons[6]. The paper declares that the State must ensure due diligence in the prevention of small arms abuses by private actors. The report goes on to state,

"While the principle of self-defense has an important place in international human rights law, it does not provide an independent, supervening right to small arms possession, nor does it ameliorate the duty of States to use due diligence in regulating civilian possession. International law does not support an international legal obligation requiring states to permit access to a gun for self-defense. The principle of self-defense does not negate the due diligence responsibility of States to keep weapons out of the hands of those most likely to misuse them".

In the U.S., the concept of private actors and their ownership of firearms continues to expand, with private actors extended ever greater legal rights to take life in circumstances that can hardly be seen as self defense. The U.S. continues to allow the possession of firearms by dangerous owners, many of whom obtain weapons without background checks, licensing or registration requirements, placing the lives of non-owners at greatly elevated risk of harm.

The extra-judicial killing of Trayvon Martin, an unarmed 17 year-old teenager by an armed vigilante is a case in point. The killer, George Zimmerman, while tried, was found not guilty, despite the lack of evidence of a compelling self-defense argument. The human rights of Trayvon Martin were clearly violated and his right to life stripped from him by the State of Florida.

Gun Regulations Do Not Produce Totalitarian States

Comparisons are sometimes made between totalitarian or authoritarian states like Zimbabwe, or North Korea and gun restriction laws. David Kopel, Research Director of the Independence Institute and associate at the Cato Institute, made this argument. His claim is that,

"Burma, Zimbabwe or Cuba...all of which, like other modern nations that are extreme violators of human rights, have extreme laws against civilian gun ownership."

A look at the laws in Zimbabwe shows that these laws are little different to those in Britain, Germany or most other European nations. Like most European nations, and most nations around the world, Zimbabwean law does not guarantee gun ownership. Zimbabwe requires a license to own a firearm, as does South Africa, which also requires a competency certificate, which Zimbabwe does not. Applicants in Zimbabwe are required to prove genuine reason to possess a firearm, as in the United Kingdom. An applicant in Zimbabwe must pass background checks, considering mental, criminal and addiction records, just as they do in Germany. Their laws are not extreme; they are common in gun laws across the world both in free, democratic societies and in tyrannical ones. Just as any oppressive regime has laws against murder, so too do democratic nations. It is neither access to nor the lack of firearm availability that makes those nations despotic, it is far more likely to be an ideological mindset.

Kopel claims that the United Nations Special Rapporteur reported that small arms are used to violate human rights, but did not report on how they are used to protect human rights. This is because these weapons are seldom used to protect populations. Across the world it is almost universally accepted that in most armed conflicts, small arms are used to assault, subjugate and oppress minorities and civilian populations. Hundreds of thousands of largely innocent people die each year in these conflicts, exacerbated by the spread of small arms. Civilians are generally seen as collateral damage or as supporters or opponents and treated accordingly. Access to small arms only serves to exacerbate and inflame conflicts, not to solve them.

Brazil: A Hub of Firearm Production

Brazil has a high death rate from gun violence, due primarily to its arms manufacturing industry, and an inability to control the number of guns in the country due to inadequate policing. The nation has between14 and 17 million guns. The gun lobby, including the NRA, pushed for greater ownership of guns before a referendum on reducing the sale of ammunition and firearms. The referendum failed and the violence continued.

Finally, in response to rising gun violence caused in no small part by the availability of firearms, Brazil introduced stricter gun laws. A rising gun homicide trend was reversed, reducing firearm related death by 15.8%, which resulted in 5,000 fewer firearm related deaths in 2010 as compared to 2003[7]. The reforms made it more difficult to purchase firearms, reducing sales from 155,834 in 2010 to 12,530 in 2012. It remains to be seen whether the decline in homicides will continue subsequent to the gun reforms.

Brazil found that it was not only necessary to implement gun restrictions, but also to reform law enforcement. However, the single most important determinant in reducing gun violence was reducing the number of firearms available to civilians. It was also determined that while popular myth had it that most crime guns are imported, the fact was that most crime guns are manufactured and purchased legally in Brazil.

It was also found that law enforcement was targeting the wrong source of firearms, due to a lack of available data. This secrecy on the part of local government and arms manufacturing prevented law enforcement from targeting locally produced and purchased revolvers and semi-automatics. Combined with inadequate gun restrictions, gun violence was kept high in Brazil to support local arms dealers. As in the U.S., the arms industry donates large sums to national and local politicians, which ensures widespread gun availability and generally lax laws[8].

Canada: More Restrictive and Far Lower Gun Deaths Than Its Neighbor

Canadian citizens have limited access to firearms. In 2009, the death rate was 0.5 per 100,000 as compared with 3.3 in the United States. The rate of private gun ownership is 23.8 firearms per 100 people, relatively high in comparison with other OECD countries. In Australia, there are 15 guns per 100 people, compared to 101 in the United States. The rate of gun homicides relates directly to gun ownership in those countries, with the United States leading the way, followed by Canada and far behind, by Australia.

In Canada, subsequent to the passage of bill C-68, firearm deaths declined dramatically from 1125 in 1995 to 816 in 2002. The firearm homicide death rate fell from 3.8 to 2.2[9]. Discussions often center on the cost of implementing the firearm bill rather than on the cost savings and reductions in loss of life. Yet, the bill cost C$100m to implement and reduced firearm injury costs by C$2.1Bn. The debate was successfully reframed from the rights of gun owners to the public right to safety. In contrast to the United States, Canada had a substantive debate that weighed the right to possess firearms against the massive loss of life and injuries caused by firearms. That debate has yet to happen in the United States.

The Canadian courts have consistently ruled that possession of firearms is a privilege, not a right, and that everyone, not just gun owners, has the right to life, liberty and personal security. Gun owners have a privilege, just as car owners do, and that with that comes responsibility and accountability[10].

Canadian gun owners continue to fight against gun restrictions despite the successes in keeping gun violence low. After the massacre in Montreal in 1989 in which 14 women were killed, gun restrictions including long gun registration were introduced. Gun owners continued fighting against these restrictions, and finally succeeded in having the long gun registration system repealed. Quebec was able to retain their registration records. It remains to be seen whether the backward step will result in higher gun violence[11].

Canada has a GPI (Global Peace Index) score of 1.31, almost half that of the U.S., ranking eighth of 158 countries measured making them a far more peaceful nation. While the gun lobby claims that Canada is more violent, the GPI does not accord with that claim[12]. While guns are prevalent in Canada, they are far more tightly controlled than in the U.S., and it shows in homicide figures.

South Africa: How the World's Most Violent Nation Reduced Gun Violence

South Africa came out of the change of power in 1994 in the wake of the apartheid regime with a disastrous gun-related death rate. Many of these guns were left over from the guerilla war fought by the military wing of the ANC, *Umkonto we Sizwe,* mostly AK-47's that had been manufactured by gun manufacturers in the old Soviet Union and China and distributed to revolutionaries around the world.

There were 26,834 homicides in South Africa in 1994. Since the introduction of the Gun Control Act of 2000, the death rate is now down significantly, with the number of homicides declining to 15,940 in 2012[13]. The percentage of non-natural deaths caused by guns since 1999 has fallen from 30.6% to 17.4% for close relationships, and from 33.6% to 17.2% today. The percentage of non-natural deaths by stabbing and blunt force trauma has remained quite constant, clearly demonstrating the positive effect that anti-gun-violence legislation has had on gun homicides. The gun homicide rate fell from 28.8 per 100,000 in 1994, to 17 per 100,000 in 2007. That translates into a decline from 11,134 homicides, to 8,319 deaths in 2007[14].

The fall in the rate of gun homicides in South Africa appears to be accelerating. Between 2007 and 2009, the percentage of gun related homicides to all homicides fell from 45% to 33%. Gun ownership has halved from 12.7 per 100 people in 1998 to 5.6 per 100 people in 2011.

Between 2004 when South Africa introduced strict gun regulation and 2012, gun crime fell 21%. A police spokesman said,

> "Tougher controls on the ownership, possession and use of firearms have seen a marked reduction in the incidence of gun-related crime in recent years. Gun control is accordingly at the heart of the ministry's strategy to combat violent crime"[15].

Serious crime per 100,000 fell from 5,287 in 2003/4 to 3,608 in 2011/12, the period during which far stricter gun regulations were implemented, another indication of the success of those restrictions in controlling crime in South Africa[16]. The five-year period between 2003 and 2008 saw a 25.8% decline in crime, a dramatic change in this very violent nation.

The South African Gun Owners Association (SAGA) disputes the figures. They claim that the data do not show whether the guns used were legal or illegal. Insufficient data were available to determine whether deaths or injuries were caused by legal or illegal firearms. However, since the reduction in overall legal firearm ownership, fewer thefts of firearms were reported. With fewer legal firearms ending up in criminal hands, the gun crime rate has also dropped. Either way, the decline in legal firearms leads to a decreasing number of gun crimes. If it is more difficult to obtain weapons legally, it will be more difficult to obtain them illegally. SAGA spokesman Martin Hood said that there is no way to link the Firearms Control Act with any specific crime. This is true, no more than we can link any specific case of cancer conclusively to smoking. We can study the overall effects of smoking on cancer and conclude that those people who smoke are more likely to get cancer. Similarly, we can conclude that if gun crimes fall significantly with the implementation of gun restrictions, those controls plainly had a tangible impact on crime in the absence of any reasonable alternative explanation.

It is true that without significantly detailed data it is difficult to conclude that the decrease in gun crime was due directly to the Firearm Control Act. We can conclude, however, that crime did not rise spectacularly as predicted by the pro gun lobby in the United States. The fact of the matter is that violent crime dropped dramatically. No area in South Africa experienced a rise in violent crime. In addition, gun crime has dropped more significantly than crimes with a knife and other violent crimes. It is prudent to conclude that guns are at the root of the violence in South Africa.

Dr Naeemah Abrahams and others at the Medical Research Council's Gender and Health Research Unit found that the use of guns as a cause of non-natural death of South African women almost halved between 1999 and 2009[17]. During the same period, deaths from stabbing and blunt injuries barely budged. If the gun rights crowd were correct that people would just find other weapons to take life, the stabbings and blunt trauma would have experienced a dramatic increase. Clearly, that did not happen.

A study of mortuary data shows that 29% of non-natural deaths in South Africa were due to firearms in 2002, this figure fell to 10.8% in 2008[18]. Yet, death from stabbings and vehicular deaths remained stable during the same period.

As a South African, I know personally how difficult it was living in a country where so many people were armed, especially with assault weapons. The chance of being shot was vastly higher than anywhere in the developed world, which is one reason I left. Having to live in a country, the United States, where an increasing number of guns are in many homes takes me back to those dark days in South

Africa, living with the fear of crime and violence. The people of both countries deserve better.

Israel: Misrepresented By the Gun Lobby

The gun lobby sometimes uses Israel as an example of a nation with high gun ownership and low gun deaths. In comparison to other developed nations, Israel does not have a high rate of gun ownership, at only 7.3 per 100 people.

A policy of reducing adolescent firearm availability in the Israeli Defense Force led to a significant 40% decrease in deaths by suicide. Much of this was related to suicide deaths over weekends. The relatively simple policy of reducing access to firearms appeared to lead directly to the decline in suicide deaths[19]. A similar reduction in suicide rates was detected in Switzerland after reforms reduced the availability of firearms nationwide[20].

In Israel, the rate of gun death is high by European standards; in 2009, it was 1.86. Firearm homicides are also high by European standards, at 0.94 in 2009[21], yet far lower than the United States. Applicants for a gun owner's license must prove genuine reason to possess a firearm, for hunting, self-defense or sport[22]. Applicants must be over 27 years of age to apply for a firearm, or 21 for ex-military service members. Applicants must pass background checks, which consider health, mental and criminal records. Gun owners must reapply and re-qualify for their firearm license every three years. Additionally, only limited quantities of ammunition are permitted for personal possession.

All firearms in Israel are registered, including acquisition, transfer and possession, and retained in an official register. Gun makers are required to record the movement and storage of all firearms and ammunition. Firearms are identified, and authorities use tracking and tracing procedures for those weapons. In comparison with the United

States, Israel's firearm laws are extremely restrictive, which accounts for its far lower death rate.

Again, as in Switzerland, firearms in Israel are tightly controlled, which calls into question the gun lobby's claims about other countries gun regulation laws.

Once an Israeli is licensed, he or she may own only one firearm, with a lifetime supply of 50 bullets that cannot be replenished[23].

Gun ownership in Israel is nothing like that in the United States, with far more controls and restrictions, and hence lower death and injury rates.

Japan: Poster Child for Gun Restrictions

In Japan, serious violent crime is almost non-existent. Japan has some of the most stringent gun restrictions anywhere on earth. It is a crime to own a firearm, yet another crime to own unlicensed ammunition and a third crime to fire a handgun. Criminal offenses have fallen every year since 2002. In 1995, there were 42 gun homicides, a rate of 0.03[24]. In 2008, there were 11 homicides with guns. The United States had more than 1,100 times as many gun homicides in that year. This clearly shows that criminals do not obtain weapons in a nation where weapons are banned. It is infinitely more difficult for criminals to get guns in Japan than it is in the United States, where there are few reasonable gun restrictions. This results in almost no gun homicides, a record that the United States should aim for, so to speak.

There is no right to own a gun in Japan, and gun ownership is a privilege. People must demonstrate a compelling reason to own a firearm. Guns are almost impossible to obtain in Japan[25], with even air rifles and shotguns difficult to get. In order to qualify for either a rifle or shotgun, applicants attend an all-day class and pass a written test, held once a month. In addition, the applicant must pass a shooting range class. Once that is confirmed, you must obtain a mental and drug test to file with law enforcement. Finally, a rigorous background check is done before you qualify. Once in possession, firearm and ammunition must be stored separately and police must be notified as to the firearms' location. A police inspection of the weapon is required every three years.

Despite the gun lobby's insistence that if guns are banned, only criminals will have guns, Japan shows that this is just inaccurate. Even the dreaded Yakuza, the Japanese Mafia, does not use firearms as a matter of course. When gun crime does happen, it is usually gangster-related, and police crack down hard on the offending gang. This shows the tremendous success of gun regulation in that country, and the dramatic impact it could have on firearm deaths and injuries in the United States. It is an ironic travesty of justice that in the country that invaded American territory and much of the Pacific, firearm death and injury is non-existent, while in the country that defeated Japan firearm deaths are among the highest on Earth. Similarly, in Germany, also defeated by the United States, firearm deaths are extremely low in comparison with the victorious nation. The disarmament of both nations by the Allies was clearly an overwhelming success.

The Japanese laws possibly hearken back to the campaign to disarm the Samurai. These self-styled warlords often acted with impunity, taking life as and when they deemed it necessary, particularly with commoners that showed them disrespect[26]. There is the very real danger in the United States that we will head down that increasingly dangerous road, with life becoming cheap and gun owners given the right, as with the Stand Your Ground laws, to kill at will.

Some people in the United States, notably David Kopel, author of a study on Japanese gun regulation, calls Japan a police state[27]. If reducing gun violence to the point that 30,000 lives might be saved each year in the United States, which translates to over 1 million saved lives over three decades, then the United States desperately needs a police state. In Japan, the police, while armed, almost never use their weapons. It seems to me that the United States bears more resemblance to a police state, given the propensity of its law enforcement to break down doors, use stun grenades on people and shoot before questioning suspects. Compared to this, Japan's law enforcement is a pussycat. David Kopel, like much of the gun lobby is somewhat prone to hyperbole in his pronouncements.

The Peaceful Far East

Most nations in the Far East, like Taiwan, Singapore, Hong Kong and South Korea have similar firearm related outcomes as does Japan. Each nation listed, if Hong Kong is counted as a nation, has low gun ownership rates, strict gun laws and low gun homicides. As with the various states in the United States, the fewer firearms in society per 100,000 population, the fewer firearm deaths. Taiwan has 4.4 firearms per 100,000 and a firearm homicide rate of 0.6, whereas Singapore has an ownership rate of 0.5 and a homicide rate of 0.02. Hong Kong and South Korea have gun ownership rates so low that their gun homicides are almost non-existent. There is little or no gun trafficking in those countries and illegal firearms are not the problem that they are in the U.S. or Central and South America. None of these nations is a tyranny or authoritarian state; all are democratic, peaceful nations.

Australia: The Courage of A Conservative

Being from Australia, I've never touched a gun. It's so not a part of our culture **(Emily Browning)**

Australia introduced strict gun regulation laws after the Port Arthur massacre in 1996, in which thirty-five people were killed and twenty-one wounded. The man, who had a history of violent and erratic behavior opened fire on tourists and shopkeepers with two semi-automatic rifles. The weapons he used were bought from a dealer without having the required firearm license. John Howard, the Conservative prime minister, forced the states to adopt the National Firearms Agreement. The agreement banned all semi-automatic rifles and semi-automatic and pump-action shotguns. A restrictive system of licensing and ownership control was introduced, supported by more than 85% of Australians, with some farmers and sports shooters being opposed[28]. The gun homicide death rate declined from 0.57 in 1996 to 0.11/100,000 in 2011. The overall homicide rate in Australia was 1.2 compared to 5.48 in the United States[29].

The Australian people decided that gun ownership was unwarranted and there was significant pressure on gun owners to give up guns in buyback programs by the government and by popular demand. It became socially deplorable to own and use guns, a reaction from which the United States should learn. Gun ownership should become as socially undesirable as smoking is today.

John Howard was advised by his security team to wear a bullet-resistant vest under his shirt at public hearings held to explain the changes, which was criticized by the pro-gun community. Some gun owners applied to join the Liberal Party of Australia; a shameless and fraudulent attempt to influence the outcome of the vote, but were barred from doing so.

Under the agreement, the government began a scheme to buy back guns from gun owners. The government introduced the Medicare Levy Agreement Act to finance the buy backs. They destroyed more than 631,000 weapons, semi-auto .22 rimfires, semi-automatic shotguns and pump action shotguns. In the state of Victoria, about 3% of firearms destroyed were military style semi-automatic rifles[30]. According to other sources, 659,940 weapons were smelted in the Australian National Firearms Buyback, with the total number of firearms destroyed exceeding one million[31].

The annual deaths resulting from firearms dropped from 516 in 1996 to just 188 in 2011, the period during which guns were strictly controlled. The rate of gun deaths fell from 2.82 in 1996 to 0.86 in 2011[32]. This evidence shows that gun regulation does precisely what it is intended to do. The rate of firearm homicides dropped dramatically because of concerted government action, an unlikely outcome in the United States. A report from the Australian government indicates that the proportion of firearm homicide victims to all homicides fell by 18% between 1996 and 2010.

Gun suicides in Australia fell from 22% of all suicides to 7% of all suicides[33]. While the number of overall homicides declined, the rate of gun homicides declined even more sharply. Before 1997, firearms were used in 24% of all homicides, whereas, in 2007, only 11% of homicides involved firearms.

Gun restrictions worked just as they were supposed to in Australia, despite the irresponsible claims from the NRA and Australian gun groups that the controls have not worked. The death rate by gun has dropped significantly, and many lives that would otherwise have been lost were saved. The risk of dying by gunshot declined by more than 50% in the sixteen years subsequent to the bans.

In 2002, an international student killed two students at Monash University in Victoria, Australia, using pistols acquired as a member of a local shooting club. As a result, gun laws were again strengthened. Ammunition clips were restricted to 10 rounds or less, a caliber limit of .38 or less, barrel length limit of not less than 120mm for semi automatic pistols and 100mm for revolvers. Stricter probation and attendance limits for sporting target shooters were also required. The government compensated those from whom it took weapons, also offering compensation to target shooters to give up the sport.

Gun deaths in Australia have continued to fall despite their already low level. Gun regulation has been spectacularly successful in Australia at preventing unnecessary deaths. While gun deaths had been falling in Australia before 1996, the introduction of gun restrictions saw deaths fall at an accelerated rate[34]. Homicide rates in Australia remain far below those in the United States, at around 0.1 per 100,000[35]. By that measure, firearm homicides are 32 times higher in the U.S.

The NRA claimed in 2000 that violent crimes had increased in Australia because of these new gun laws. The Australian Federal Attorney General Daryl Williams accused the NRA of falsifying government statistics and urged the NRA to remove any reference to Australia from its website[36]. The NRA claimed that assaults involving guns rose 28%, gun murders increased 19% and home invasions climbed 21%. The group claims that "Australian government crime statistic reports are dishonest, incomplete and inconclusive because they focus on the method used in a small sample of homicides and suicides or make correlations between a piece of legislation and an accompanying drop in figures[37]". Australian Attorney General Daryl Williams had this to say about the NRA claims,

> "I find it quite offensive that the NRA is using the very successful gun reform laws introduced in 1996 as the basis for promoting gun ownership in the United States."

While some claim that Australian gun regulation cannot be shown as the cause of the reduction in both homicides and suicides in Australia subsequent to the introduction of gun restrictions, there are other indicators. The drop in firearm deaths was greatest among the types of firearms most affected by gun buybacks. States with higher buyback rates saw greater falls in firearm deaths than those with lower rates. There was no evidence that other methods of either homicide or suicide were substituted for firearms. The rates of total firearm death, firearm homicides and firearm suicides all doubled the rate of decline after introduction of the gun laws[38]. The rate of decline in suicides exceeded 80%.

Dr. Adam Graycar director of the Australian Institute of Criminology said that in 1998, assaults had indeed risen, but that most did not involve guns. Homicides had decreased and rarely involved guns. Graycar said that it is difficult to attribute the change in crime directly to the new gun regulation laws, since there are many factors at work, such as changes in demographics.

John Howard, the former Conservative Prime Minister of Australia has come out publicly in favor of continued gun bans in Australia, and believes that the United States needs to get rid of its guns. He said that firearm homicides in Australia have dropped 59% between 1995 and 2006, while there has been no offsetting increase in non-firearm related murders. In the 18 years before the 1996 Australian firearm laws, there were 13 gun massacres resulting in 102 murders. Since the introduction of gun restriction laws, there have been none[39], in stark contrast with the United States. Since 1982, there have been 62 mass shootings in the United States, and the numbers seem to be increasing[40].

A study at Monash University in Victoria, Australia, studied mortality data between 1979 and 2000 that included unintentional death, assault, suicide and other firearm related deaths. Their conclusion read as follows,

"Dramatic reductions in overall firearm related deaths and particularly suicides by firearms were achieved in the context of the implementation of strong regulatory reform".

In other words, gun regulation succeeded in reducing the levels of gun death[41]. Another period studied concluded that in 1988 after gun reforms in Victoria following a mass shooting, firearm deaths declined 17.3% compared to the rest of Australia where gun deaths remained relatively constant.

The SSAA (Sporting Shooters Association of Australia) continues to fight sensible gun laws that have been instrumental in reducing gun violence and death in Australia. With their ideology melded to that of the NRA, they cannot accept that gun restriction works to the betterment of the people of Australia, the fact that gun restriction works as intended not withstanding. They would rather have unfettered access to firearms than see substantial reductions in death and injury.

United Kingdom

The gun industry often uses the United Kingdom as a poster child for what happens when countries introduce gun regulation measures. They make the claim that subsequent to these constraints, violent crimes rise in number.

Gun proponents abuse statistics to claim that violent crime in the UK is higher than in the U.S. This produces a conclusion based on dissimilar statistics. Violent crime as measured by the FBI Uniform Crime Reports lists murder and non-negligent manslaughter, forcible rape, robbery and aggravated assault as violent crimes[42]. In contrast, the British Crime Survey (BCS) includes simple assault, robbery, sexual offenses, and non-sexual emotional or financial abuse as violent crimes, leading to substantial differences in the way crime is counted. British statistics for violent crime are listed with and without injury[43].

Over the five-year period ending in 2013, violent crime in the UK has fallen by 21%. Offenses such as public disorder fell 29%, weapons crimes dropped 34% and homicides are down 28%. The absence of guns appears to be working as a factor reducing violent crimes, not increasing them. Muggings and pickpocketing have risen, feasibly since car theft and burglary are more difficult to accomplish successfully. Incidences of reported rape have risen, possibly since women are less reluctant to report having been raped. The odds of being murdered in the UK is at its lowest since 1978[44].

The UK Peace Index, a measure of the relative peace in a society shows the rate of violent crime falling. In 2012, violent incidents fell 12% from the year before. The crime rate per 100,000 fell from 1,255 to 933 in 2012 and 833 in 2013, more rapidly than any other European nation[45].

According to the UKPI, homicides as a proportion of total violent crimes are almost 10 times higher in the US than in the UK[46]. The report claims that access to guns in the U.S. contributes to the high rate of gun homicides. The UK is one of the most peaceful countries on Earth as measured by the Global Peace Index, ranking 29th of 158 countries measured, an improvement from 48th in 2007.

Police officers in the United Kingdom, unlike their contemporaries in the United States do not carry firearms[47]. There is no need for them to do so, considering the low level of gun violence in the UK. In the US, almost all active duty police officers carry a personal sidearm, often a Taser, and other self-defense devices. There have been only 68 police officers killed in the UK in 110 years "*as a direct result of a crime or while attempting to prevent, stop or solve a specific criminal act*"[48]. In the United States, 169 officers died while on duty in 2011 alone. In 2012, 47 officers were killed because of gunfire, double the number killed in automobile accidents[49]. The U.S. deaths in a single year by gunfire alone amounted to two thirds the number of officers killed in the UK in more than a century, while in 2011, almost three times as many officers were killed.

The British police authority to carry firearms was revoked in the 1980's because of the deaths of a number of members of the public at the hands of armed officers. Today, most officers go unarmed, but there are Armed Response Vehicles used in specific circumstances. The law enforcement authorities in the UK consider their relations with the public to be more important than carrying firearms. This is in stark contrast with the U.S., where members of the public are routinely killed by police officers, often in atrocious killings such as that of Amadou Diallo. Diallo was an unarmed, 23 year old migrant from Guinea who was shot and killed by four New York police officers in 1999. The officers fired 41 shots, 19 of which struck the immigrant, killing him[50]. All four officers were exonerated of guilt, despite the excessive force used and the complete absence of probable cause.

The prevalence of guns in the U.S. creates a culture in which police officers expect members of the public to be armed, and react accordingly, leading to the killing of unarmed men, often African American. As elucidated in the book *"Above the Law: Police and the Excessive use of force"*, U.S. law enforcement inhabits a nation under siege, beset by a culture of urban warfare, a mindset of us versus them. According to one unofficial estimate, in the first half of 2012, police, security guards and self-appointed law enforcers killed 120 people, mostly unarmed African Americans. Only 8% were ever charged with the killings[51].

The Global Peace Index (GPI) shows that Western Europe is the most peaceful, violence-free region on Earth today. Considering that there are few firearms in comparison to the United States and more gun regulation laws, it is clear why that might be. The overall GPI score of the United Kingdom is 1.79, compared with 2.13 for the United States, making the UK a more peaceful region than the US.

Switzerland

Gun regulation in Switzerland is categorized as restrictive. The U.S. gun lobby would consider the gun laws in Switzerland "tyrannical". All able bodied males must have arms, as part of their national military conscription; however, these arms are used as part of a national militia, not as private weapons. They are issued either a 9mm pistol or an assault rifle during their service. The assault rifle is converted to semi-automatic by removal of the rapid-fire function. These firearms must be kept in the home or at a local armory[52].

Up until 2007, ammunition was issued, sealed and inspected regularly by Swiss authorities. This ammunition was intended for use only while traveling to army barracks in the case of invasion. After October 2007, all ammunition issued was ordered returned. Only special rapid deployment units and military police still have ammunition issued today. Switzerland still has a high number of gun homicides relative to the rest of Europe; in 2010, that rate was 0.52[53]. In comparison, the rate in the U.S. is seven times higher.

After military conscription ends, a serviceman may apply to retain his assault rifle, which is subject to licensing and the completion of two federal programs. Ammunition for rifles is available at shooting ranges and subsidized by the government, but the ammunition cannot leave the range. In addition, the rifle is modified from semi-automatic to single shot before being handed over[54]. A service member may keep his pistol without licensing or range qualification. In addition, all weapons are registered and the details of the owner retained for a period of 10 years.

While Swiss citizens can possess firearms by law, no automatic firearms, some automatic firearms converted into semi-automatic firearms, no incendiary, armor-piercing ammunition or expansive projectiles for handguns are permitted[55]. For some manual repetition rifles, there is no licensing requirement, but in most cases, only licensed owners may possess, acquire or transfer a firearm or ammunition[56].

Many in the American gun lobby point to Switzerland as an example of a nation with a large proportion of armed citizens and low violence. In reality, Switzerland has a far higher rate of gun death than any of the developed nations on its borders, including Germany, Italy, Austria and France. In Europe, the association between increased gun ownership and gun death rates correlates closely. Switzerland, like Finland, which also has a high rate of gun ownership, experiences high levels of gun death and injury.

Switzerland has a gun ownership rate 7 times that of the United Kingdom, and a gun death rate 15 times that of the U.K. Some claim that rates of violence are not high in Switzerland, which may well be true, but their rate of gun death is definitively higher than European nations with stricter gun laws.

Clearly, firearms are closely controlled in Switzerland, as is ammunition. The large number of guns in the country does lead to a higher death rate than the rest of Europe, but the control of firearms keeps the death rate far below that in the United States where controls are often either indifferent or non-existent.

Debunking the Pro Gun Argument

If guns don't kill people, why do mass killers arm themselves with guns?
(DaShanne Stokes)

I'm for gun control. I'm a peace-loving guy. **(Arnold Schwarzenegger)**

Many conservatives, members of the gun lobby and others argue that the high death rate by gun in the United States is the price we pay for "liberty". In their minds, liberty represents the right to own firearms regardless of the harm that those weapons do. By extension, then, the death of children to gun violence is part of the gun owners right to carry firearms. Seldom do they pay homage to the rights of those who have died, to their liberty, to their lives. Life, the ability to live rather than die is the ultimate liberty, the ultimate freedom in a world in which death is all too easy, in which there are more ways to die than there are to live. Yet, gun owners insist that their right to liberty supersedes the rights of the one million Americans that have died through gun violence since 1980.

Most developed nations around the world, especially in Europe are just as "free" as the United States is, given their democratic freedoms, and they do not need firearms to ensure that freedom. They have the right to speak freely, to vote for their representatives, to move from place to place; in Europe, people can move between countries without hindrance, a liberty not recognized in the Americas. Europe has not been overrun by dictatorships or authoritarian regimes, nor do they live in fear of law enforcement. The gun lobby in the United States insists on the right to bear arms to prevent their government from imposing an authoritarian regime, but other countries have not recently experienced these situations.

Voter supported gun buybacks and firearm amnesties happen in Democratic societies, not authoritarian or tyrannical regimes. Nations including the United Kingdom, Canada, Australia, Brazil and Argentina have all introduced stricter gun laws and buybacks, with startling success in reducing gun violence[1].

People Won't Obey the Law

Gun rights advocates claim that lawmakers are concentrating on law abiding gun owners and not enough on criminals. In reality, all laws target both law abiding and criminal elements of society. We have road laws not to target those that drive safely, but to ensure the safety of all. The intent of law is to proscribe the safe, moral and ethical manner in which society must comport itself. It is only once people attempt to contravene those laws that they are indulging in criminal behavior.

Law abiding people should have no problem adhering to laws intended to make society a safer place in which to live. Laws are written to show people that certain behavior is not allowed, and that if contravened, there are penalties to be paid. If we had no laws regulating murder, rape or robbery, people would steal, take lives and force sex on others with impunity. With the laws in place, law-abiding people know where the boundaries are, and understand that their actions may result in severe criminal sanctions.

Responsible people know that laws are there to protect them and society from the actions of criminals or those with violent intentions. The fact that certain gun owners and the gun industry want no laws at all shows their contempt for the law and for the safety of society. If we were able to trust that people are responsible, we would not need laws at all to govern societies. It is naïve to expect people to believe that the mere ownership of firearms makes people responsible. Since too many people are incapable of being responsible, society makes laws to protect itself. That is the basis of the law.

Those who choose not to obey the laws are committing either felonies or misdemeanors. While there may be unreasonable laws, or poorly conceived laws, they are laws nonetheless and we obey them for fear of the consequences. In democratic societies, we can change our representatives in order to change laws with which we disagree. Until that time we have little choice but to obey those laws.

Comparing Guns to Automobiles

Since 1937 when the rate of motor vehicle deaths was 29 per 100,000 people, the death rate has declined steadily to its current rate of 10 per 100,000. We have produced safer automobiles, speed limits, safer roads, traffic lights, and vehicle safety features, mandated by the federal government. At the current rate of decline in auto deaths, the 30,000+ annual gun deaths will likely exceed the number of road deaths nationally by 2015[2]. Regulation of roads, vehicles, drivers and traffic flow has led directly to this success. The same cannot be said of the firearm industry - we have yet to duplicate this success with sensible gun regulations. The death rate per 100,000 was 10.19 in 2000 and 11.96 in 2016, showing that the rate is rising, not falling. When we regulate automobiles, the death rate falls, and yet we cannot do the same with firearms. As a result, within two or three years, the death rate from firearms will likely exceed that from motor vehicle accidents.

A motor vehicle has a purpose, which is to transport people from one place to another, which it does quite efficiently. Given the enormous number of road trips each year, a certain number of people do die, but these are mostly accidental deaths, not intentional homicides or suicides. With vehicles, we test them for safety; build in new safety features, give them ratings for highway safety, and introduce laws restricting what drivers may do. With guns, rather than mandate safer firearms, we expand the categories of extremely dangerous weapons that people may possess, where they may carry them, produce ammunition that is more lethal and accessorize to increase their range and lethality. If we treated weapons like cars, we would have more restrictions, improved laws and fewer deaths.

Gun advocates sometime make the claim that cars kill people too, yet we do not ban cars. This is untrue; many vehicles are not allowed on public highways. Vehicles driven on Nascar circuits are not allowed on public highways, construction vehicles are transported to their worksites and not allowed on roads. Vehicles on the roads are regulated in terms of headlights, indicators, catalytic converters, fuel type, tire type and a host of other restrictions. In addition, there are speed limits, traffic lights, stop signs, driving on the right, and reduced speed for certain traffic conditions.

Each year, vehicles travel a total of 3.03 trillion miles, for the 254.4 million vehicles on the road[3], and this number is increasing as people drive more vehicle miles each year, and the death toll declines. As long as people are at the controls of vehicles, there will be accidents. What we try to do as a society is mitigate that number, and do whatever possible to reduce deaths and injuries. This is in stark contrast with the gun lobby, which steadfastly stands in the way of regulations that would save lives.

Just as society has intervened to address automobile deaths and injuries by addressing the agent, which is the vehicle; the host, which is the driver; the environment, which is the roadway, so society can address the death rate by firearm in a similar way. We can study and produce sensible regulations for the instrument, which is the firearm, introduce licensing, registration and insurance for the gun owner and the society by improving infrastructure, and raising the standard of living[4]. The intervention by government in the vehicle injury sphere is spectacularly successful. There is no reason that the same dynamic cannot be applied to firearms.

An Armed Society is a Polite/Peaceful Society

An armed society is a polite society. Manners are good when one may have to back up his acts with his life. **Robert Heinlein.**

A society in which certain people are armed and others are not may be a polite society, but that politeness is drawn from fear and wariness, not from decency or morality. People are too afraid to stand up for their rights if they feel that their lives may be in jeopardy, as witness, the Stand Your Ground laws in many states. Many nations with authoritarian regimes are polite societies because of the fear of the regime; the same goes in the United States where greater numbers of people are armed.

Research shows that people who possess arms are more likely to make obscene gestures at other motorists while driving[5], or drive in an aggressive manner, such as tailgating. Males, young adults, binge drinkers, those who do not believe people can be trusted, those arrested for traffic violations and motorists in a vehicle with a gun are more likely to indulge in these behaviors.

Many gun owners see themselves as the knight in armor, using their firearm for the greater good, Sir Galahad in modern garb. This is the John Wayne mentality, the idea that evil lurks in the world and it is their responsibility to seek it out and purge society of those malevolent forces. They see themselves as protecting weaker members of society. Yet, firearms are used to kill 105 people each day, and murder 39. There was no chivalry there, no knight in shining armor, no Lone Ranger, despite the 300 million guns in private hands across the U.S., just base homicide. Few people are protected or defended by armed civilians with guns; far more people are killed or commit suicide.

Many gun owners see themselves as protecting their wives and children and perhaps a neighbor, yet statistics show that firearms in the home are far more likely to be used to threaten, coerce, assault and kill members of the household than they are to be used in self-defense. While some may believe that guns transform them from

Clark Kent to Superman to help the helpless, a firearm is far more likely to be used against an unarmed member of the public than in his, or her defense.

A peaceful society is one in which both people and animals can go about their business without a fear of death. Superman would not use an assault weapon to kill dozens of deer, rabbits or coyotes; he is the man who rescues kittens from trees and helps elderly people across the road.

Considering the inordinate degree to which people die from firearm violence in the U.S., as compared to other countries, a true Samaritan would destroy all personal firearms in society. Other nations manage to keep their gun deaths low; there is no reason that we should not.

The public display of firearms becomes the bully's paradise, a way to swagger and strut in public, and intimidate others without the need for overt brutality. Given the Stand Your Ground laws, bullies can kill with impunity and walk away without charge. That is not a polite society; there is nothing polite about firearms. In a polite society, people would have no need to shoot one another, or to carry firearms. A society that takes to the gun has lost the ability to be polite or civil. Saying an armed society is a polite society is really an oxymoron; the presence of arms implies the lack of good manners.

If guns create a polite society, given the 300 million guns in private hands in the U.S., the country should be more polite. When a massacre happens, some gun proponents become so angered, threatening to "start killing people" if gun regulation goes "one inch further", as Tennessee CEO, James Yeager, said in a YouTube video[6]. If guns create a more mannered society, gun proponents do not need to demonstrate in the streets with fully armed assault weapons, often in an overtly threatening manner, as happened during a peaceful protest by Moms Demand Action.

Gun proponents have been told that some people are intimidated by firearms like assault weapons, yet they insist on demonstrating in a manner that many see as threatening. A truly polite, civil society would understand that while you may believe that you have rights, the one thing you do not have is the right to force them on others. Taking weapons into a public space is an explicitly brazen and threatening gesture to many.

If gun owners believe that their firearms create a civil society, they should not feel the need to threaten insurrection when there is any talk of gun restrictions. Since there is no talk of taking guns away, only of placing minor restrictions on ownership of certain weapons, yet they supersede the bounds of civil discourse and courtesy by threatening violence. The only reasonable conclusion is that guns do not create a civil society; *ipso facto,* they create a discourteous one.

The fact is that those with the means to do so historically always perpetrate violence against those without such means. It is no different in the U.S., the most armed society on Earth. The fear of violent death at the hands of those who are armed is at the core of the desire for gun restrictions. A polite society would surely recognize that the peaceful and the unarmed should have the right to live peaceful lives without coercion from those with firearms. Clearly, civility is not at the forefront of the minds of those who bear arms.

Armed Men: The Mark of Tyranny
Political power grows out of the barrel of a gun: **Mao Zedong**

There are plenty of societies around the globe that allow armed civilians in the streets, and none of them are stable, developed democracies. Every one is a nihilistic state on the brink of lawlessness, with law imposed arbitrarily by those with arms, and with those arms comes the power of the gun. Civilians who are not armed live in fear for their lives; fear that something they do, or say may raise the ire of those who are armed. Life in those nations is cheap, and the continued introduction of laws legitimizing murder, such as Stand Your Ground, and Shall Issue laws forcing states to allow anyone to buy arms, is making life here ever cheaper.

We as a society must live in fear of gunmen with concealed weapons in shopping malls, restaurants, bars, churches, schools, and government buildings. We are safe nowhere, never free of the presence of powerful weapons. We may as well live in Somalia or Zimbabwe, with their contemptible indifference to life. The gun lobby pushes for open carry everywhere, anywhere, at any time, in any circumstance, and guns bought without background checks or restrictions.

Wayne LaPierre recently said that more guns equal more safety, yet the facts do not concur. More guns in this nation have brought nothing but misery or death to the 32,000 people who die each year, the 70,000 to 80,000 who are injured, and their families. Other societies are far safer, and often far more polite.

They mistake politeness for obsequious supplication, people's deep suspicion that they might be victims of the gunman's wrath. Guns project power and the fear of that power; the result is not politeness, it is apprehension and anxiety. What guns have taken from us is our right to a civil society, to the peace of a society in which law enforcement and democratic institutions are the guarantors of our liberty, and not unbridled vigilantism.

The threat of violence that accompanies firearms, and this threat becomes more ominous the more powerful and visible the firearm, is a way to manipulate populations, to control them, to communicate the threat or intent of violence. This is how nihilistic, violent societies ensure the compliance of the people. Increasing the firearms on the street only detracts from societies' freedom of movement, and destroys true liberty.

Guns do nothing to enhance the freedom to speak, to assemble, to be disputatious or contentious in a public setting. Their presence is a damper on free speech, the right to argue, to display displeasure, for any sign of annoyance or antagonism could end in the morgue. When we are not free to disparage, to mock, to insult, we are not free.

Thus, the possession of arms, especially assault weapons and even more so in the public space is an impediment to the free exercise of ideas and as such, a violation of the noblest and finest Amendment to the Constitution, the First. The Second Amendment as interpreted by the gun lobby and the Roberts court, is no more than an insolent rupture in the flow of the Bill of Rights, and is being used to shred the rest of the Constitution.

While gun advocates claim that any restriction on firearms are the actions of a despotic government, the mere presence of increasing numbers of firearms in the public sphere in essence creates an atmosphere of despotism and tyranny. If power springs from the barrel of a gun, government, by allowing the free ownership of firearms, is controlling those who do not possess arms through those who do.

According to an editorial in the New York Times, America now has the dubious distinction of having a greater number of armed guards than high school teachers, more than one million in all[7]. Including law enforcement, armed forces, prison and court officials, military contractors and weapons production, almost 5.2 million workers are now involved in the security sector. Gated communities, doormen and security devices have proliferated over the last few years. This has become a society under siege, in which security is necessary to protect the privileged few from the ravages of armed violence. No other developed democracy needs to resort to the securitizing of its society in order to be safe. The people of this nation spend more on protecting themselves than on otherwise productive pursuits, which is the consequence of ubiquitous firearms.

The ubiquity of firearms in the public space ultimately results in the disintegration of the community bond, as each gun owner becomes in essence his own law enforcement body, with his own set of rules; the ultimate nihilistic state and a recipe for shredding of the social contract as society becomes more fragmented. Instead of feeling secure in public, since each person might be armed, we become less secure, less a part of that society, and fearful of everyone.

Crime Deterrent or its Means

The gun lobby claims that having everyone armed is a powerful deterrent to criminals, what they don't say is that those who are armed may be the criminals, that we are putting arms into the hands of people we may not be able to trust. We have no reason to trust gunmen in our public spaces; they have not demonstrated that they are indeed trustworthy. People who possess firearms, especially the most extreme firearms, are far more likely than average citizens to be schoolyard bullies, abusers in intimate relationships, people who resort to violence to resolve problems rather than peaceful people. Having a firearm clearly benefits the criminal in an armed society, especially one in which firearms are universally available.

Politicizing Tragedies

In the wake of each gun massacre in the U.S., pro-gun advocates immediately accuse gun regulation advocates of politicizing the tragedy. They call for a period of mourning, for the nation to overcome its grief and let the surviving victims overcome their emotions. In most developed nations, a gun massacre is a time for reflection, a time to discuss whether firearms are too easily available to people.

In the wake of the Dunblane School Massacre in Scotland, the United Kingdom had a serious discussion about the private ownership of handguns. After the gun massacre in Port Arthur, Australia, the country introduced stricter anti-gun-violence laws despite heavy opposition. In Canada after the killings at the École Polytechnique, new regulations on guns were introduced after an intense debate about guns. Other than the vitriolic reaction from the gun lobby, those countries did not implode; rather the discussion resulted in rational restrictions on firearms. In the United States, we are not allowed to talk about implementing these rational controls for fear of politicizing a tragedy. The same restriction does not appear to apply to the gun lobby, especially the NRA, which uses each tragedy to sell more firearms.

When Hurricane Katrina hit New Orleans, and again after Hurricane Sandy hit New Jersey, the discussion was about preparing for another large storm, protecting the shoreline, and whether to move houses back from the beaches. The discussion was not considered political. The same should be said about gun regulation. Immediately after a tragedy, when the tragic images are still on people's minds is precisely the moment to talk about gun restrictions and how to mitigate gun violence. There is no better time, for people's memories are short and they will move on to other things all too soon.

Not talking about the tragedy is itself a strategy with a political motivation, and that motivation is to postpone a debate until people no longer remember the tragedy, or its impact has vanished as people accept the loss. If we had waited forty or fifty years to talk about the Holocaust, few would remember it today. That we did not, kept the tragedy alive and forced people to acknowledge it and implement strategies to ensure that it would not happen again. Attempts to ignore the tragedy only amount to a repudiation of responsibility, to disregard or invalidate the incident to gain political advantage.

There is no better way to honor victims than to work relentlessly to ensure that the victims were not lost in vain, that society will do everything it can to correct systemic failures and make the world a safer place.

Gun advocates do not want to get close to a gun massacre because of the intense spotlight it shines on their possessions. The NRA, as the shining star in the gun industry's arsenal wants only to keep its head down, and when it comes out, to attack everyone else as being to blame for the tragedy. An honest, open debate is the last thing they want, since it brings their most fervently held beliefs into focus, requiring a defense.

Claiming that a tragedy is being politicized creates a poor impression of anti-gun-violence advocates and puts them on the defensive, as though they were perpetrating an offensive act, and taking the spotlight off the tragedy and the gun industry. What is always lost is the horror of yet another gun massacre. The correct time, for the gun industry, to talk about gun massacres and gun regulation, is generally, never. They do not want an honest debate; they want to sell more guns to more people, regardless of the consequences.

In the wake of tragedy, it is not helpful to target those who pushed these weapons on a vulnerable population, and nor should we right then. The object of the exercise is to target failed policies and rectify them. In the case of firearms, the deregulation of firearms has led to too many deaths, and the industry needs to be re-regulated. If the gun lobby sees that as political, let them make that argument. In the meantime, the nation needs real adults in the room who are going to make the tough choices to get guns out of the wrong hands.

Gun advocates use every tragedy to induce people to buy more firearms, to protect themselves from the phantom barbarian hordes invading their homes each day. Every massacre is an opportunity to instill even more paranoia in their acolytes and get them to prepare for political, social or economic Armageddon. This is the most cynical political exploitation of tragedy, enriching the gun industry while people still mourn those they have lost. Gun restriction advocates want to tackle the underlying cause of gun violence, which amounts to gun overload, while proponents want ever more instruments of death to flood the streets.

Year in and year out, the NRA, ALEC, Gun Owners of America and others, politicize guns, by demanding that legislators do their bidding, put more guns in the hands of those who should not have them, and yet when it comes to tragedies they make possible, we cannot politicize it. The message is that they can do it, but when we experience the consequences of their actions, of the guns they have pressed on people, we cannot politicize it. A small, vocal minority pushes dangerous firearms on the population, regardless of consequence, and because they are so focused and vocal, they get their way, while a complacent population does nothing.

In the absence of a substantive gun regulation debate, the steady drumbeat of death and tragedy continues, decimating poor communities, sentencing spouses or children to abuse, violence and death, while we experience more random, senseless killing. Few politicians have the courage to stand on principle and say, "get rid of the guns, restrict ammunition purchases and assault weapons, put in background checks, for people cannot be trusted with instruments of death".

For the gun lobby, when President Obama paraded the families of the victims of Newtown before the cameras, it was politicizing the tragedy, as though the victims' families had no right to demand that something be done about gun violence. They deserve a hearing; their tragedy was real enough. The gun lobby appears to believe that they should hide until the storm is over. The families of Newtown, Aurora, Columbine and others, are clearly expected to sacrifice their loved ones to the Gun Deity and keep silent about their loss. The gun lobby can exercise its academic Second Amendment right, but the victims' families cannot exercise their First. We expect our leaders to lead in times of crisis, to comfort, but also to take substantive action as swiftly as feasible, and it is no different for the incessant gun massacres and anonymous gun deaths plaguing our society.

Tragedies have struck relentlessly in the four years since President Obama took office, and each time the country mourns, shakes its gory locks at the inexplicability of it all and refuses to politicize it, or to talk about it, for we must honor the dead. We honored them while the gun industry was selling more guns. We honored them while Congress held their palms out for baksheesh from the gun lobby. There were no victims' lobbyists, tame Congressmen and advertising executives. For a president who was going to take everyone's guns from them, the gun problem has only grown worse, and people continue to die by the score each day.

By not politicizing tragedies, Congress and the gun industry ensures that the victims of the tragedy receive no justice, and that nothing is done to change the status quo. Our society, and its leaders, is failing in its duty to protect vulnerable victims by ensuring that guns do not fall into the wrong hands. Not politicizing these tragedies is in itself a political act, a repudiation of responsibility, and a callous disregard for the victims. This ought to be known as the Ostrich Congress, sticking its head in the sand and hoping that the predatory gun owner wont notice. Imagine if, after the attacks on Pearl Harbor, we had said lets not politicize this moment, it is a moment for reflection and mourning, lets wait a few months and then talk about it. Today, we would all speak Japanese. After a tragedy, the right time for action is immediately.

People Can Kill with Other Weapons

Gun rights groups sometimes make the somewhat spurious claim that if guns were not available, people would find other weapons with which to commit criminal acts. This may or may not be true, depending on circumstances.

Firstly, the reason a firearm is so dangerous in the wrong hands is that it is so easy to use and difficult to undo. Pulling a trigger does not require great strength, dexterity, thought or planning. Due to its relatively high velocity and stopping power, depending on a number of factors, among which are the velocity of the projectile, the size of the projectile and the distance over which it is fired, it is likely to cause tremendous damage to soft tissue, bone, or other body parts.

Knives, clubs, fists or feet are more commonly used in street fights than are firearms. The difference is that a firearm endows its possessor with the ability to quickly escalate and intensify the level of violence to the point that fights and disagreements are far more likely to be fatal. Society has an interest in ensuring that violence do as little damage as feasible; the most effective way to accomplish this is to keep highly destructive weapons out of the hands of civilians.

A person with little physical strength or skill can cause significant damage to an adversary using a firearm. Compare that to any other weapon, lets say a knife; the odds of damage are significantly greater with a firearm. With a knife, the possessor must have relatively greater skill, know which body parts to target and penetrate the defenses of the opponent successfully. It can take significant force to do harm to a victim in order to penetrate bone and flesh, which is relatively simple with a firearm. The knife must be used in close quarters, with the victim given warning, which may not be the case with a firearm. Firearms can be used at distance, without endangering the shooter.

The same can be said of any blunt instrument that may be used on a victim. The assailant must be close enough to use the weapon and possess sufficient strength and skill to do damage to the victim. A club takes strength to use effectively and penetrate a victim's defense. Violent crimes with guns are about 3 times as deadly as crimes with knives and 44 times as deadly as crimes committed without weapons[8]. Gun violence is the single most deadly driver of homicide in the U.S.

The human arms race has moved in a direction that ensures that weapons become more effective at killing greater and greater numbers of opponents. The defense forces of the world issue their soldiers automatic and semi-automatic weapons with good reason. Clubs, knives, arrows, swords or darts are entirely ineffective if opponents are armed with automatic weapons; consider the ease with which the European colonial powers subdued vast areas of Africa. As President Obama so succinctly put it, we no longer issue our troops with bayonets, for the most part, because they are ineffective.

Firearms have evolved over time from the first invention of gunpowder, for good reason. As time passed, modifications in the production of firearms has made them more reliable, easier to use, and more effective at killing, which is their ultimate task. Firearms have evolved through the matchlock gun, rifling, flintlock, percussion principle, back action lock, revolver, pin-fire cartridge, rim-fire cartridge, repeating carbine, breech loaders, Gatling guns, Winchester rifle, double action revolver, automatic handguns and so on[9]. As they have evolved, they have become easier to use, maintain, clean, more accurate, more powerful and thus more effective.

One article I found, and there are hundreds of articles in similar vein, had this to say,

> "Much like the military, civilian AR shooters are on a never ending quest for improvements in accuracy, reliability and comfort.[10]"

We should not allow civilians to look for increasingly more effective ways of killing. Society has an obligation to all its citizens to ensure that they are safe from more effective killing machines.

That is why most societies limit the weapons a civilian can use; we as a society do not want civilians owning more efficient killing machines. The terrible slaughter at Sandy Hook Elementary was possible only because of the effectiveness of the weapons the killer used. The more restrictions on the weapon, the fewer innocent lives he would have been able to take. If he had been limited to a revolver, for instance, it would have been far more difficult for him to commit the terrible atrocity in Newtown.

It is intellectually dishonest for pro gun groups to claim that in the absence of firearms, criminals will choose other weapons. Few mass killings by an individual are committed with anything other than firearms. The massacre of Tutsis by Hutus in Rwanda was carried out predominantly with machetes because firearms were expensive, but many were slaughtered using rifles[11]. The Hutus used their superior numbers, armed with firearms, to block off villages and massacre the residents. This was not the action of a single individual in a university able to carry out multiple murders with an assault rifle.

It is true that Timothy McVey used chemical fertilizers to destroy the Alfred P. Murray Federal Building in Oklahoma City, but the ingredients for explosives cannot be purchased on every street corner. It takes specific knowledge to produce and successfully use explosives, and a great deal of planning and preparation. Guns are easy to use, require no specialized knowledge, and are available everywhere.

Gov. John Hickenlooper, of Colorado now believes that gun regulations ought to be tightened. After the tragedy in Sandy Hook Elementary, the governor said[12],

> "the time is right to ask such questions as do we need assault weapons. When you look at what happened in Aurora, a great deal of the damage was from the large magazine on the AR-15 rifle".

Yet, his comments were rather different after the tragedy in the Aurora Theater in which he said,

> "I worry that if we got rid of all the guns, and certainly we have so many guns in this country, the shooter would have found explosives…or poisonous gas..he would have done something to create this horror".

Other than the Sarin gas attack on the Tokyo subway, I have yet to find any evidence in this country or any other of an attack using poisonous gas. Explosives are common in countries at war, but are seldom used in peaceful nations. In the mass killings in this country, other than the attack on the Alfred P. Murray Federal Building in Oklahoma City, explosives are almost never used. Guns are far more common. The killer in Aurora had access to guns and that is what he used. Had he not had access to those weapons, it is far less likely that he would have been able to carry out his attack.

Not only that, supplies of ammonium nitrate, as used by Timothy McVeigh in his attack on the federal building, are now monitored by the federal government. It would be difficult for anyone without training in explosives or chemistry to obtain the ingredients necessary to produce explosives. The dearth of attacks using explosives is evidence that common sense gun restrictions actually do prevent attacks. It may not prevent every one, but it does make it far more difficult for people to obtain the necessary ingredients, which is precisely why we should have gun regulations.

States are not implementing gun restrictions in some part because of the belief that killers will find a way to commit mass murder, and by so doing, are encouraging gun violence to continue in their states. No alternative method of killing is as ubiquitous, as easy to obtain and as easy to use, as firearms. I challenge any legislator to come up with a method of killing that is easily obtainable, legal, and encouraged by society, other than firearms.

People Die More from Other Causes

A common argument from opponents of gun restrictions is that more people die from other causes than from guns. They often cite such things as poisoning or drowning as causing more death than firearms. As with many statistical analyses, you need to define your terms before using them.

For instance, poisoning can be loosely divided between drug poisoning and non-drug poisoning. Given the ubiquity of drugs in society, there are going to be a great many deaths, especially from illicit narcotics. In 2012, there were drug-related 41,502. Non-drug poisoning, considering that we live in a society that produces more than 18,000 different chemical compounds, is quite rare in comparison. In 2012, there were 4,648 non-drug deaths; that is one seventh of the number of firearm deaths, while there were 2.5 times more homicides from firearms.

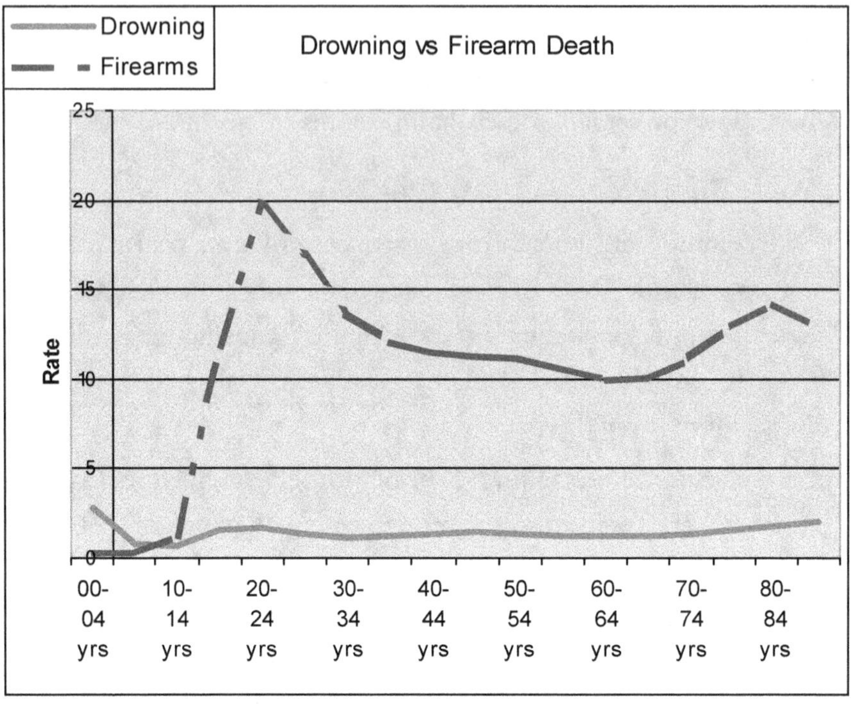

There were 4,308 drowning fatalities in 2012, around a third of the number of firearm homicides. Some critics point out that a child is far more likely to die from drowning than by firearms. Far more children are likely to be around various bodies of water, including the bath than they are around firearms. We do not encounter children running around with firearms, which accounts for the drowning deaths. As can be seen in the chart above, drowning deaths are high below the age of five, while firearm deaths exceed drowning thereafter. What is interesting is that the rate of death by firearm for children under 10 (0.37), exceeds the firearm death rate for the all population groups in the United Kingdom (0.23)

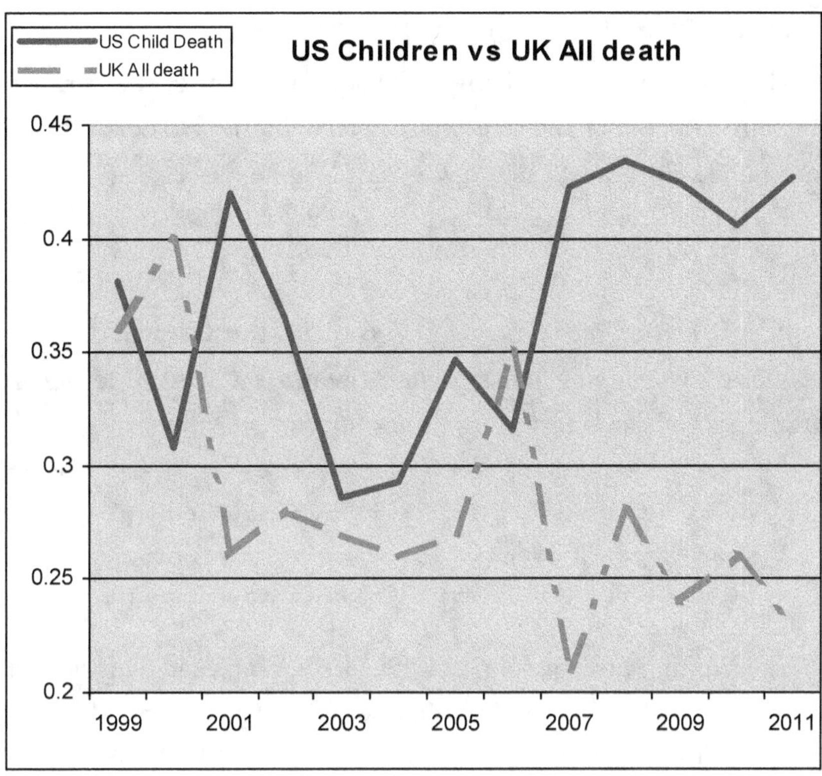

Only 986 people lost their lives due to being struck by someone, and 2,648 people died through stabbings. While society successfully expends great efforts on reducing death and injury by every cause, it spends very little on reducing firearm death and injury.

Accidental death does happen, that is part of life, but given the unnecessary deaths from firearms, our society does very little to prevent those deaths.

Even if accidental deaths are caused by means other than firearms, this is no reason to stop trying to prevent firearm death. Societies should try and mitigate death from all causes.

Gun Regulation Caused the Holocaust

The NRA makes the claim that Adolf Hitler, Nazi fuehrer, banned guns in Germany, and that this preceded the Holocaust, thereby causing the Holocaust. In the words of Wayne LaPierre[13],

> "In Germany, Jewish extermination began with the Nazi Weapon Law of 1938, signed by Adolf Hitler."

In 1919 after the Treaty of Versailles, the German Legislature passed a law banning most private firearm ownership, to adhere to Article 169 of the Treaty. This article stated[14],

> "Within two months from the coming into force of the present Treaty, German arms, munitions, and war material including anti-aircraft material, existing in Germany in excess of the quantities allowed, must be surrendered to the government of the Principal Allied and Associated Powers to be destroyed or rendered useless."

The Weimar government, not the Nazi's, confiscated most firearms in private hands, and they did this because of the terms of the treaty signed with the Entente (Allies). This was 14 years before the accession to power of the Nazi party. In 1928, the Weimar government relaxed the laws, but required registration for gun possession. In part, this was to combat the Nazi's and other groups who were threatening armed insurrection. To that end, the laws worked; the Nazi's had to rig the electoral process through intimidation in order to win an election, in many ways similar to the gerrymandering currently afflicting the political process in the U.S.

Thus, it was not the Nazis, but the Allied powers that banned firearms, which helped to prevent violent insurrection for 14 years after the Treaty. In 1923, Hitler attempted a putsch along the lines of Mussolini's successful *coup d'état* in Italy, but he failed, and was sent to prison. Arms control was therefore successful at preventing an armed insurrection. Had arms been freely available as they are in the

U.S., it is quite plausible that the putsch would have succeeded, as happened in Italy under Mussolini.

Persecution of the Jews and other minorities began long before the 1938 German Weapons Act introduced by the Nazis. The Act did not ban weapons; it relaxed controls on the ownership of firearms, except for non-citizens. The Jewish people and other non-Aryan groups were stripped of citizenship, making them ineligible to own firearms, or own firearm manufacturing. The Jewish people and others were stripped of almost every imaginable human right subsequent to the Nazi accession to power in 1933, which began long before the 1938 Weapons Act.

The right of Jewish people right to work, live, trade, petition the government, speak freely, move freely, marry and dozens of other rights were stripped from them before 1938. Guns would not have made an ounce of difference to their situation, especially against one of the most well armed and formidable fighting machines in history. Additionally, most Jewish people in Germany would not have owned firearms even had they been able to, since they were for the most part a peaceful people who had no need to own firearms.

The lack of gun regulations and sheer quantity of arms in this country leaves us vulnerable to armed insurrection, a far more frightening scenario than the arbitrary confiscation of firearms. An armed insurrection would feasibly lead swiftly to civil war and the potential death, given conservative disregard of human suffering, of millions of residents.

Gun Regulation won't Prevent Massacres

Gun restrictions in other developed countries has worked spectacularly well in reducing massacres. In Australia, in the 18 years before the Port Arthur shooting, there were 13 mass shootings. In the decade after the introduction of comprehensive gun restrictions in

1996, there was not a single mass shooting[15]. The same is seen in other countries that experienced massacres, including the United Kingdom and Canada.

No one in their right mind expects any law to stop all of anything. This is a straw man planted by the conservative gun lobby. Laws against murder, robbery and fraud do not stop any of those things, but without those laws, it is likely that there would be a lot more of them. Laws tell the people what restrictions there are on their behavior, and what punishment society metes out for disobeying those laws. That is the basis for a law-abiding society. If we institute a ban on assault weapons, we do not expect that all massacres will stop, but we do expect that many will be prevented, and that is a good start.

Similarly, with any gun restrictions, we do not expect that all murders or suicides will stop, but we do expect that there will be a reduction in them. To say that laws wont stop 100% of something and therefore we should not have those laws is disingenuous at best. It is unreasonable to expect anything to stop 100% of any crime, but that does not mean that we should not try.

What bans on certain types of weapon, ammunition or additions to weapons will do is to take those items off the street. That makes it far more difficult for people to obtain them legally, and will deter most people from trying. It also raises the cost of those items; for many criminals, cost is of paramount importance, since many cannot afford expensive weapons. The effect of removing weapons from society is seen over a number of years rather than immediately, which is what conservatives do not accept. For those groups, if a ban does not have an immediate effect, it must be a poor law. After the Gun Control Act of 2000 in South Africa, the decline in homicides and gun crimes was steady for over a decade.

A ban on assault weapons is unlikely to stop all massacres, but it may stop enough to save many lives, and that is the primary concern. Lives must always take precedence over the rights to ownership. There is a tendency on the part of some commentators to throw up their arms whenever there is a tragedy and tell us that we cannot possibly prevent all massacres and therefore it is no use trying to do anything substantive. If we tackled all our problems in this way, we would probably still live in caves, using flint to create fire and hoping that a mammoth would wander off a cliff somewhere to give us meat. We can as other countries have done, at least mitigate massacres with sensible, comprehensive anti-gun-violence laws.

Sometimes living in the U.S. is like living in a bubble; we cannot comprehend that other nations successfully tackle difficult issues like gun regulation and gun massacres. Gun regulation works in every developed country across the world with the exception of the United States. That we refuse to see the efficacy of efforts in those countries says a lot about our indifference to science and fact-based solutions.

Massacres Happen in Gun Free Zones

Of the 62 mass killings in the past thirty years, only 12 happened in schools. It is questionable whether all those schools were designated as gun-free zones. Of the rest, 20 happened in the workplace. The remaining 30 mass shootings included shopping malls, restaurants, and religious and government buildings[16].

These shootings happened in 30 states across the country, in both red and blue states. More than three quarters of the guns used were obtained legally[17].

Gun Regulation Makes Gun Owners Guilty

The ALEC initiated, "Resolution on the Second Amendment to the U.S. Constitution"[18] makes the assertion that laws restricting firearms including bans, taxation, waiting periods, registration, licensing and even confiscation assume the guilt of all firearm owners without addressing those who misuse and criminally abuse firearms.

This is rather like saying that when we make laws restricting vehicle speed on public roads, register vehicles, tax those vehicles and the fuel that they use, and insist on licensing drivers, we are assuming the guilt of all drivers. Just like drivers and their vehicles, society should be able to decide who can own weapons, under what circumstances, and how we restrict their use. Society has a right to be safe from people that either use or misuse those weapons. We should not for instance have gun owners firing their weapons in state parks or along the Appalachian Trail and elsewhere people might be walking, hiking, camping or otherwise enjoying the natural beauty of the country. Unfortunately, that is precisely what we do have.

Law-abiding people should accept that society places many restrictions on behavior that may be detrimental to others in that society, to ensure their safety, security and enjoyment. There are plenty of statutes that address criminal actions, including those laws against murder, rape, robbery, or any other action that people may take with a firearm. Those laws have been on the books for decades and in some cases for centuries.

The assumption that anti-gun-violence advocates want to confiscate all firearms is mostly inaccurate. Most gun regulation advocates only advocate small changes in current law, adding restrictions on certain types of firearm and accessories. The comparison with Prohibition in which all alcohol was banned is likewise false, since only certain firearms would be restricted.

There is no assumption of guilt, only the realization that the number of deaths by firearm each year is unacceptable and we must do whatever we can to reduce those deaths. Liberty is a fine philosophy, but not if by exercising your liberty, you take another's life, even if by proxy. Some gun owners may be law abiding and do not use their firearms in frivolous ways such as questionable Stand Your Ground incidents, but the incorrect assumption that gun owners are law abiding by virtue of their gun ownership is just another attempt to whitewash the fact of the inordinate number of deaths in this country. Clearly there are enough gun owners that are not law abiding, that thirty two thousand people are killed and seventy thousand seriously injured each year.

We cannot expect all gun owners to be personally responsible people. Some will be, some will not, and those that are not will continue to kill others with impunity, if not immunity under Stand Your Ground laws. As with any law, it is not the law abiding that we seek to cover, our concerns are the irresponsible people. Just as Stand Your Ground laws remove the restriction on murder, which raises the number of deaths, removing restrictions on firearms also increases deaths.

If comprehensive gun restrictions were introduced in the U.S., it would not instantly criminalize everyone. In Australia in the wake of the Port Arthur shooting, restrictions were placed on the purchase of new weapons. In addition, a firearm repurchase program was introduced that bought back firearms from the public. Millions of people are not instantly criminalized with the introduction of new laws; as with most laws, things are introduced gradually, or are given a period before taking full effect. Any talk of instant criminalization is just paranoia.

Banning Guns Creates Black Markets

Gun proponents claim that banning guns will make them more expensive and create black markets for weapons. This, according to these groups will result in turf wars as criminals refuse to give up their guns. Law abiding citizens will be defenseless against armed bandits. Firstly, as guns become more expensive, criminals will no longer be able to afford them. Paying thousands of dollars for a used AK-47 is just not feasible for the average criminal.

In Japan, there is very little gun smuggling because of the harsh penalties imposed for possession. In fact there is far more gun smuggling from the U.S. to neighboring states than there is in Japan. There are no turf wars, which are stamped out quickly by Japanese law enforcement. The same can be said of Europe. There are few turf wars, unlike those sometimes seen in the U.S. with its ubiquitous firearms.

Gun Regulation Creates Crime

Gun regulation does not spawn crime, as crime statistics in developed countries with strict gun restriction show. On the contrary, the ubiquity of firearms is far more likely to spawn crime. We need only study the ungovernable societies across the globe, many of which have far too many firearms in private hands.

Some gun proponents claim that we need armed civilians to prevent or deter violent crime before it starts or spreads. In civilized societies, we call that law enforcement, specially trained citizens who understand the law and the enforcement thereof and are empowered to prevent or deter crime. Adding untrained civilians is a disaster waiting to happen, as has happened with the extra-judicial executions experienced during Stand Your Ground events.

Millions of Guns are Used in Self-Defense Each Year[19]

The figure of 2.5 million self defense gun uses each year is so ubiquitous that it warrants an entire section. The figures below are from a report produced by Prof. David Hemenway, which I list in the endnotes. Professor Hemenway produced such a succinct critique of the 2.5 million statistic that it bears repeating here. It is a great shame that far too many in the media choose to repeat this figure without looking at the underlying study, or the alternative figure produced by the National Crime Victimization Survey (NCVS).

The gun industry and their lobbyists often claim that guns are used millions of times per year in self-defense. Prof. Gary Kleck, a criminologist released a report estimating that firearms were used 2.5 million times per year in self-defense[20]. Kleck conducted a survey in 1994 (The National Self-Defense Survey) that was used as a basis for his claim. The NCVS estimated in 1994 that fewer than 100,000 instances of self-defense occurred each year. This is far more than an order of magnitude below the gun industry claim. The NCVS is a survey carried out twice per year, every year since 1972; the Kleck survey was a single event, conducted in 1994.

Few studies have produced a figure approaching millions of annual self-defense uses. Gun advocates and much commentary in the media cite the Kleck survey in most testimony, without countervailing testimony from other surveys, such as NCVS. The lack of scientific rigor in the Kleck survey contrasts with the NCVS, which is conducted regularly, and includes a large survey demographic. Despite studies done by the scientific community indicating the inefficacy of firearms for self-defense, the Kleck survey is often cited as gospel.

The results of the NCVS survey, based on some 50,000 housing units found that victims use guns against offenders in self defense about 65,000 times per year. Residents answer detailed questions about various crimes committed against them. These questions are repeated every six months for three years. Only about 34 people reported having used a gun in self-defense[21]. In 2010, there were 617 justifiable homicides[22], amounting to some 0.02% of all self-defense uses reported by Prof. Kleck a decade before. It is unlikely that of 2.5 million self-defense uses, only a tiny percentage resulted in justifiable homicide. That same year, there were more unintentional gun deaths (851) than justifiable homicides.

Many reported instances of "self-defense" are against animals; in one recent instance, a man shot an endangered black bear that had wandered onto his property, despite the fact that the bear was not threatening him. The judge did not buy the claim and charged the man with an offense.

The 1995 Kleck survey was an aggregation of 13 prior surveys, few of which defined the term "use" of a firearm in self-defense. It is impossible to say whether those weapons were actually used for self-defense. It is questionable whether the carrying of a firearm constitutes self-defense, or whether the weapon has to be drawn, and whether it is used to stop an actual physical life-threatening attack. The mere threat of an attack should not constitute justification for self-defense usage. Taking a firearm to investigate a disturbance in or around the home similarly does not constitute self-defense.

Criminologist Prof. Kleck refuted the NCVS figures; he believes that people under-report uses because the survey is not anonymous, and because the survey asks only about those instances in which someone has been victimized[23]. There is no reason to undermine a survey merely because it not anonymous. If someone has not been victimized, firearm use cannot realistically be referred to as self-defense.

Prof. Kleck, in surveys taken between 1976 and 1990, used a sample size of 600-1500 to produce his results, statistically too small a sample to extrapolate to the nation's entire population. Measuring low probability events with small sample sizes can lead to significant distortion in the results. He concluded that guns were used 700,000 times per year in self-defense. The only question asked on the survey was "Have you used a gun in self defense in the past five years". In 1992, Kleck conducted a phone survey of 5,000 homes that produced the figure of between 1m and 2.5m uses of self-defense. Kleck prefers to use his survey result of 2.5m uses[24].

Respondents in the Kleck survey were not questioned again after the initial survey. There is no distinguishing between military or police uses, or uses against animals. Additionally, what some respondents may assert is self defense may actually be an overt act of aggression, sometimes mistaken for self-defense[25].

Many interviews were not completed if people were not home, and only the male head of the household was questioned. A greater proportion of white males from Southern and Western states were questioned than are present in the U.S. population. The Southern white male demographic is far more likely to own and use firearms than the rest of the nation.

People living in communities with high gun ownership rates, typically in the South and West may be susceptible to social desirability bias; that is to claim self-defense usage to impress their circle of acquaintances and to demonstrate their prescience and judgment in purchasing a firearm. Respondents may see themselves as heroic, or defending an American archetype, which may make them appear more socially acceptable in the eyes of their compatriots in the gun community. They may perceive themselves as saving the lives of a great many people each year, giving them reason to obfuscate the truth. According to their claims, hundreds of thousands of lives are saved each year[26], compared with 15,953 homicides in 2011. Any self-defense use with a firearm is far more likely to cause an injury than not, so something must account for the gap between the claims of millions of uses and the reality of several hundred justifiable homicides.

Many gun owners are aware of the debate over guns and self-defense, giving them a compelling reason to want to improve the statistics in favor of gun defense, and to support a political ideology. This may give them a compelling reason to exaggerate. Based on Kleck's survey, at least 1,166 of the 88,800 people surveyed in the NCVS survey must have been lying about not having used a gun in self-defense[27]. This seems unlikely, since only 34 people affirmed using a firearm in self-defense. Kleck presented no compelling evidence in support of his contention that the NCVS survey is incorrect other than his own personal bias.

While Kleck claims that guns were used 34% of the time against offenders during burglaries, the Atlanta police department found that of 198 burglary cases, only three victims were able to use a firearm in self defense. Hemenway calculates that since there were 6m burglaries in 1992, the building was known to be occupied only 22% of the time, fewer than half of Americans have firearms and two thirds of victims were asleep at the time, firearms would have to be used by burglary victims more than 100% of the time[28].

According to Kleck, of the 500,000 cases of rape, including attempted rape, sexual assault and verbal threats of sexual assault, guns were used in self-defense 205,000 times[29]. This amounts to some 40% of rape cases[30]. Very few rape victims are likely to use firearms in self-defense; especially since only about 10% of women own firearms and far fewer would be in a position to use a firearm during rape. If Kleck were correct, there would certainly be more gun shot victims during rapes, whether the victim responded to the rape, or the rapist took the firearm from the victim.

Furthermore, Kleck claimed that gun owners believe more than 1.15 million lives either would, might or probably have been killed had a firearm not been used in self defense. Given that fact, Hemenway calculates that it is likely that hundreds of thousands of murders would be happening each year if people were not armed. Since the actual homicide figure is about 1% of that, this scenario is highly unlikely[31]. This is especially true in areas of the country with few firearms - homicides are not dramatically higher than in those areaas with many firearms; on the contrary, firearm deaths are far more rare.

The report states that around 207,000 times the gun owner believes that he either wounded or killed the intruder. In 1993, only about 100,000 were treated in emergency rooms for non fatal firearm injuries, mostly for assault, suicide and accidental shootings, not criminals shot by intruders[32]. Again, the Kleck statistics do not accord with publicly available facts.

The statistics used to this point were all taken in 1992/3. The NCVS for 2011 comes to a similar conclusion. The nonfatal firearm crimes in 2011 amounted to some 467,300, and of those incidents, only 1% of victims reported using a firearm to defend themselves[33]. That amounts to some 4,600 times per year, even without the likely false positives. This is nowhere near the 2.5m claimed by Kleck in 1992. If we take into account the drop in gun crimes from 1.5m, we can estimate 1.7m uses of firearms for self-defense based on Kleck's claims. That still does not accord with the 4,600 times reported on the survey. Even if people did not report self-defense uses during victimization, that still does not account for the discrepancy between the two figures. At least 61% of nonfatal firearm violence was reported to law enforcement.

The Kleck surveys also suffered from a confirmation bias as pointed out by another critique[34]. According to this critique, the National Self Defense Survey (NSDS) survey carried out by Kleck did not attempt to count defensive gun use by law-abiding citizens. *"No attempt was made to determine the lawfulness or morality of the defensive actions"*. The surveys also did not "compare the effectiveness of armed resistance with other forms of victim self-protection". The Kleck surveys also admitted that they encouraged *"the reporting of acts that were extremely sensitive and legally controversial"* and that some of the acts could be construed as "unlawful assault" and even that possession of the firearm *"might itself be unlawful"*.

Property crime victims reported using a firearm in self-defense 103,000 times, about 0.1% of all victimizations[35]. This figure still does not accord with the estimated 1.7m self-defense uses claimed by Kleck. Around 85% of victims of property crime were not present during the incident.

Perhaps the single most troubling aspect of the Kleck study is that there are no corroborating studies conducted by gun proponents to verify his findings. While John Lott did a certain amount of research, it is the Kleck study, carried out in the early 1990's when the gun violence rate was at its height, which is cited almost across the board. No recent studies have been carried out, especially considering the dramatic declines in gun violence since 1993. In contrast, the NCVS surveys, using a far more substantial population segment are carried out each year, and have been since their inception. Self-defense incidents, even if close to the Kleck study, must have fallen in parallel with the decline in gun violence.

The 2.5m statistic is sometimes used to justify possessing firearms for self-defense. If, as is demonstrated, the figure is wildly inflated, that removes the justification for ownership of firearms for self-defense. Using a firearm for self-defense is a low probability event, and given the dangers of guns in the home, it is more dangerous to the inhabitants of a home with firearms than to an intruder. This argues strongly for removing firearms from homes for any purpose. It should be clear that it is safer to live in a home without a firearm than in one with firearms. Self-defense thus cannot be used as a justification for the possession of firearms.

Violent Crime Declining While Guns Increase

Violent crime appears to be declining in the United States, despite the increase in the number of guns available. Since 1991, when the murder rate in the United States was 9.8, the number of murders has dropped significantly. Criminologists have proposed a number of reasons for the decline: improved police tactics; changing demographics in an aging population; the change in the drug trade; the Clinton initiative to hire more police officers; and legalized abortion, since fewer unwanted pregnancies resulted in fewer children becoming criminals. There is also the fact that more Americans than ever are serving time in prison, with the prison population at 753 per 100,000, 240% higher than it was in 1980[36].

Levitt[37] finds more support for improvements in law enforcement, increased incarceration rates and rising prison population, the decline of the crack epidemic and the legalization of abortion. By this token, the current drive for austerity measures, which include cutting back on law enforcement, may well result in increased levels of overall crime and especially gun homicides. The increasing tendency of conservative states in the South, Midwest and Mountain West to restrict access to abortion could also serve to increase the rate of violence. The short sighted attitude toward local and state policing could well have the effect of increasing the costs to the community in the increased need for first responders of all kinds to respond to shootings, robberies and other violent crimes.

The insistence by Republicans, that social programs are harmful to the recipients, is probably false, given that the removal of assistance may lead to increased levels of crime and violence. This reduction in assistance may be one factor responsible for an increased number of deaths and injuries by gun, and the failure of public policy prescriptions by Republicans. In addition, an obsession with phantom terrorism has diverted resources away from community policing and exacerbated the already unacceptable levels of gun homicide.

Some suggest that tactical policing and the decline in crack cocaine may be contributing factors in the reduction in crime[38]. Some researchers have also found a connection between reductions in childhood lead poisoning because of the use of unleaded gasoline, improved substance abuse prevention and an expanded public assistance safety net as factors in the decline of overall gun crime[39,40]. Austerity measures, and a refusal to tackle substance abuse problems with anything other than incarceration, in the United States, may ultimately reverse the trend toward fewer gun homicides.

The gun lobby claims that violent crimes are declining due to an increase in gun ownership. Violent crime is dropping around the world, in both countries with guns and countries without. The most controversial reason given for declining crime is a drop in the use of leaded gasoline. Lead in gasoline is a highly toxic compound that may affect the development of the nervous system during infancy; infants exposed to lead appear disposed to violence and aggression[41]. Guns thus appear to have little to do with the decrease in crime. We need to question whether the drop would be faster in the U.S. if there were lower rates of gun ownership.

In Japan, criminal offenses have dropped every year since 2002[42]. Japan has one of the lowest levels of crime on earth, and strict gun restrictions. In South Africa, gun homicides have dropped significantly since 1994, which marked the end of the apartheid era. Cities across Canada, Europe and the U.S. experienced a marked drop in crime between the 1980's and the 1990/2000 periods. This gives the leaded gasoline hypothesis some credibility, and negates the belief that an increase in firearms precipitated the declines.

Reductions in leaded gasoline appear to explain the differences in crime between large and mid size cities. Since there is a greater concentration of vehicles in large cities, leaded gasoline can make a significant difference in lead found in infants. Subsequent to the introduction of leaded gasoline, homicides in large cities declined from 35.5 in 1994 to 11.9 in 2008. The drop in cities with populations between 100,000 and 250,000 was more modest, declining from 15 in 1994 to 8.8 in 2008. Gun ownership does not appear to have been a factor.

In 2001, violent crime was seen to be increasing in the United States[43], due probably to slowing economic growth, a shift away from social support programs, a shift in policing towards terrorism and a slowing rate of adult incarceration[44]. Gun homicides actually increased for males 25-44 in large central and metropolitan areas.

Declines in homicide may also be due to increasing use of the justice system to resolve disputes rather than violence. As political institutions improve and people's rights are observed more strictly, people see less reason to resort to firearms for personal protection. The trend in the U.S. is currently away from greater rights and towards a more nihilistic society in which many believe, wrongly, that they need more self-protection. Ironically, while the world becomes more peaceful, with less violence, Americans want more guns to defend themselves from violence. By so doing, they are increasing the risks and likelihood of violence, which would seem to justify the possession of firearms.

Gun homicide rates are dropping in concert with the downturn in homes reporting guns, which may also explain declining levels of crime. In states like Montana, New Mexico and Wyoming, homes reporting ownership dropped from 65% in the 1970's to less than 40% today. In the Northeast, ownership fell from 29% in the 1970's to 22% today[45].

Gun ownership particularly among the young is declining dramatically. Among those under 30, the rate more than halved from 47% in the 1970's to 23% today. The rate among Republicans has actually risen from 47% in the 1970's to 51% today, while among Democrats and Independents, there was a steep decrease in ownership rates between the 1970's and today. In rural areas, the drop is from 70% in the 1970's to 56% today, while in urban areas, only 23% own firearms[46]. The rate among women has remained constant at about 10% since the 1970's while among men it is over 30%.

As of 2006, 38% of households and 26% of individuals own at least one firearm[47]. This translates to 42 million households and 57 million adult gun owners. Men are more likely to own a firearm, with 45% admitting to owning at least one handgun. 48% of individual gun owners owned more than four weapons.

Even in the South and Mountain West, gun ownership has declined from 65% in the 1970's to less than 40% today. In the Northeast, the most peaceful part of the country, ownership is about 22%.

Some claim that Americans want to hang onto their guns, and yet the current surge in gun purchases appears to be restricted to existing gun owners, especially among the elderly. Republicans, who appear to experience higher levels of paranoia about crime and their government, continue to have high levels of gun ownership.

According to an article published in the Wall Street Journal, despite the decline in the national homicide rate, the injury rate due to firearms is rising dramatically., in 2001, 20,844 people required hospitalization for gun shot injuries. By 2011 that figure increased by 47% to 30,759. Trauma surgeons are more effectively treating gun shot wounds. Where people would have died before, they are now surviving gunshot trauma[48]. The CDC reports that nonfatal gunshot injuries requiring hospitalization numbered some 26,897 in 2001, rising to 41,300 in 2012, a rise from a rate of 9.19 to 13.16. This translates into a 53% increase in hospitalization injuries. However, given small sample sizes, those estimates may be unstable.

Other Nations Have Gun Massacres

The gun lobby claims that gun massacres in other countries proves that gun regulation does not work. Their argument is similar to this; since those countries mostly have gun regulations and cannot prevent every massacre, we should not restrict guns at all. Like many arguments against gun regulations, this one is another *non sequitur*.

We have laws against many crimes, murder, rape, fraud, robbery, and none of them stops any of those offenses. What they do provide is a guideline for society. You can commit murder, but you if you are caught you will be punished. If you are caught robbing a store, you will go to jail, and so on. Laws tell people what they can and cannot do. Laws also restrict what products are available to people.

If we take away people's ability to purchase firearms, they will find it far more difficult to commit violent crimes with firearms. In countries with strict gun regulation, gun violence is almost non-existent. People may commit crimes with other weapons, but it is far more difficult for them to kill large numbers of people without firearms.

There are still some tragedies in other countries, but at a far lower rate, commensurate with the ability to obtain firearms. In many countries, the risk of gun shot death or injury has vanished entirely. In Japan, 2007 was a particularly bad year for gun deaths. They had twenty-two deaths in that year, which caused a national scandal, as opposed to two the year before in 2006. In 2008, there were 11 deaths[49].

Clearly, gun regulation works in Japan, as it does in other developed nations. In 2007, some Japanese people were asking whether Japanese traditional values had changed[50], because of the dramatic increase in gun deaths. That was over 22 deaths, which happens over a slow weekend in Chicago or Atlanta. We need to ask whether American traditional values should include random shootings as part of the culture. Japanese culture is not morally superior to our own.

The gun lobby cites the mass killing by Anders Breivik in Norway as evidence that other countries with stringent gun restrictions also have gun massacres. Breivik purchased $550 worth of 30-round ammunition clips from an American supplier for the rifle with which he killed 69 Norwegian children at a camp for the Workers Youth League (AUF) of the Labor Party.

Breivik spent six days in Prague, Czech Republic in an attempt to purchase firearms, believing that Prague had the most relaxed laws regarding guns and drugs in Europe[51]. He hollowed out the rear seats of his vehicle to make enough space for the weapons. He wanted to buy an AK-47 to use in the attacks, but he was unable to purchase them in the Czech Republic, and concluded that it was not an ideal city to buy firearms. Instead, he purchased a semi-automatic rifle and

Glock pistol legally in Norway, noting that he had a clean criminal record, hunting license and two guns. He obtained a legal permit for a .223 Ruger semi automatic carbine for hunting deer. He had wanted a 7.62mm Ruger mini-30, but gun laws fortunately prevented his obtaining it. Getting the pistol proved more difficult because of Norway's gun regulations, and he had to attend a pistol sport-shooting club regularly in order to qualify.

Glenn Beck, noted conservative TV host, and NRA member, compared the AUF camps to the Hitler Youth. It is uncertain as to why his belief that these children had a tenuous connection to the Hitler youth justified mass slaughter. He claimed that the youth camp bore "disturbing" similarities to the Hitler Youth[52]. Beck has a series of schools that he terms "vacation liberty schools" in which children as young as eight are taught religion, economics and political principles. This appears to bear at least a passing resemblance to the Hitler Youth.

If Norwegian gun regulations had not been as loose as they were, Breivik would not have been permitted to purchase his weapons, and 69 children would be alive today. In addition, he was able to purchase ammunition clips from an American supplier, which if unavailable to him would have prevented the slaughter. Again, the American system contributed to the slaughter of these children by allowing for the purchase of these ammunition clips by a foreigner. Breivik's experience in Prague shows that when it is difficult enough to purchase firearms, massacres are less likely to happen.

Very few gun massacres happen outside the United States, or in comparison to the United States. Over the past 30 years, there have been some 62 mass shootings in the U.S. After each mass shooting in other countries, gun restrictions were introduced, subsequent to which gun massacres do not occur. This phenomenon is true in Canada, the

United Kingdom and Australia, all of which experienced gun massacres in the late 1980's or 1990's. Subsequent to the introduction of gun restrictions, massacres evaporated and gun crimes declined, despite already low levels of gun violence.

In stark contrast to the United States, other developed nations have the political courage and fortitude to stand up to vocal gun proponents and introduce sensible laws. Australian Prime Minister John Howard put his own political career in jeopardy as he pushed through tough gun legislation. The results since 1996 have been remarkably successful in preventing further massacres. Gun related homicides in Australia dropped 59% between the Port Arthur massacre in 1995 and 2006. Additionally, gun suicides dropped almost 80% with no effect on non-firearm death rates[53].

In the UK after the massacre in Dunblane, Scotland, tough gun restrictions were introduced, resulting in successive years of declining gun violence. It certainly has not prevented gun violence; in 2010, a taxi driver killed a dozen people in Cumbria[54], but there have been no other massacres in the years since Dunblane.

Most Gun Deaths are Suicides not Homicides

As I have pointed out before, there were 32,163 gun related deaths in the United States in 2011. Of those, 19,766 were suicides, and 11,101 were homicides. Critics of gun restrictions use these figures to claim that since suicide does not involve violence to others, it should not be counted when talking about gun violence.

Suicide is most definitely a violent death; the fact that it is self-inflicted does not change that. Without universal firearm availability and the ease with which guns are obtained there would be fewer suicides. Simple changes to the law to include universal background checks for all gun trades would go a long way to mitigate death by suicide. Correctly managed, many people with Severe Mental Illness, or others who may be vulnerable to suicide could be prevented from purchasing firearms. Similarly, a simple waiting period may well prevent a large proportion of those suicides, since many suicides are spontaneous acts, often carried out within a few hours of purchasing a weapon.

Suicide also has a dramatic impact on families, communities and anyone witnessing or experiencing the outcome of a gun suicide. Just as a death sentence for murder affects not just the families of the victim, but the family of the perpetrator, suicide can devastate a family, plunging them into poverty and depression. Just as murders have a profound effect on communities, the same can be said of suicides.

The dismissal of suicides as an aberration of little consequence accentuates the indifference to life displayed by gun proponents. We as a society should understand the despair that can drive a person to suicide and attempt to mitigate it as best we can, by for instance improving our mental health system, and taking guns away from people who may be a danger to themselves.

The idea that 11,000 homicides each year is a better statistic than 32,000 is yet another gun lobby deception. In comparison with other developed nations, the figure is vastly higher than it should be. The United States has a firearm homicide rate of 3.6 per 100,000, which is 7.2 times higher than Canada, 27 times higher than Australia, and 60 times higher than the United Kingdom[55].

Banning assault weapons, high capacity magazines, and regulating gun shows may not have a direct impact on suicide, but they address a gun culture that glorifies violence, or for some, violent solutions to societal problems best handled by law enforcement or the judicial system. It is only by tackling the prevalence of firearms that we can start to reduce gun violence.

NICS Background Check System Does Not Work

The NICS or National Instant Criminal Background Check System allows for the checking of people buying firearms through licensed dealers. The system is currently plagued with problems that include missing data. Some states do not provide information to the system, which allows prohibited persons to slip through the system. The shooter in Virginia Tech, Seung-Hui Cho was able to purchase firearms, since his mental health information was not in the system[56].

It is up to Congress to ensure that the system is fully funded and has all the information required to make a solid determination about a purchasers eligibility. The NICS Improvement Act of 2007 authorized $1.3 billion in grants funding state agencies and courts. The system has actually received only about $50 million since 2009[57]. Even President Obama only wants to increase funding to about $20 million. This is nowhere near enough to fund the program. Gun advocates cannot credibly claim that the system does not work if they refuse to fund it.

Background Checks: A Burden on Purchasers; Amount to a Gun Registry

The background check, using form 4473 takes minutes to complete and imposes no realistic burden on purchasers. The overwhelming majority of Americans, currently around 84%, believe that there should be a background check to purchase a firearm[58].

While gun proponents claim that background checks allow government to create a gun registry, the truth is that all records are destroyed within 24 hours of purchase. The Manchin-Toomey gun proposals put forth in the 2013 session of Congress specifically reinforce the prohibition of a gun registry. Congress has gone above and beyond to reassure gun proponents that a gun registry will not happen, despite it being a rational step to take.

Conservative circles are rife with conspiracies that a gun registry will be imposed upon them whenever gun legislation enters the public sphere. With revelations about the NSA and domestic spying, some conservatives are convinced that the NSA has already created a gun registry. Given the vast amounts of data collected not just by intelligence agencies, but also by corporations, any authoritarian government will have little difficulty obtaining any data it desires about a person's life. Gun ownership would likely be the least of their concerns. Authoritarian regimes like the National Socialists in Germany in the 1930's were far more interested in a person's political affiliation, sexual predilections or religious proclivities than their gun ownership.

There are compelling reasons to create a national registry, and most developed nations have one in place. The government and the people have a right to know who is in possession of highly destructive weapons for any number of reasons. When law enforcement is sent to deliver a warrant, to question suspects or witnesses, or government workers are sent to conduct the census, they should have the right to know whether they are placing their lies in danger by stepping onto a resident's property.

In the event of insurrection, patriotic citizens need to know who is trustworthy and who is not. The idea that people retain firearms as a bulwark against tyrannical government is little more than seditious. In a free and open democracy, no rational resident plans insurrection against his own government. Residents who own anywhere up to a few dozen firearms, including assault-style weapons, and considerable quantities of ammunition, present a clear and present danger to a democratic state, or to any state.

Residents should also have the right to know who in a community poses a threat to their lives, and make residential choices accordingly.

We have registries of sex offenders, who pose far less of a threat to life than do people possessing highly destructive weapons, and we make those records freely available to the public. When we choose where to live, we should be aware of the dangers of living in that community, such as nearby chemical or nuclear plants, water or air pollution, driving hazards and whether our neighbors are armed with assault weapons. On that basis, we can decide where to reside.

Registration itself would pose no direct threat to anyone's purported right to bear arms. The belief that a registry enables government to seize firearms is little more than paranoid delusion.

In a delicious irony, recent revelations brought to light the fact that the NRA itself has a secret registry of gun owners[59]. There is no difference between government keeping such records and a private organization doing the same. That information might easily be passed to an administration or to other interested parties and used to target gun owners. It could also be co-opted by an administration for its own use. Instead of a government, accountable to the people having a list of gun owners, the United States now has a private organization that is not accountable to the people, keeping secret lists. That poses a far greater threat to liberty than does a gun registry.

The NRA compiles its list using gun permit registration lists from state and county offices, gun safety classes taught by NRA instructors, attendees of gun shows, and subscribers to gun magazines[60]. Yet, when a newspaper published details about gun owners in two New York counties, the NRA was outraged at the violation of privacy. The organization even offers to buy lists of concealed permit holders from police departments as it did from the Virginia State Police.

In some states, prospective gun owners are compelled to take classes from NRA-certified instructors, giving those people no alternative but to divulge their details to the NRA. When government does this, the NRA claims it is dictatorial, yet when the NRA does it, it is considered freedom.

These lists are used to convert gun owners into dues paying NRA members, and to contribute to the NRA Political Action Committee. Gun ownership is a key determinant of individual political inclinations. We can only imagine the response if anti-gun-violence groups obtained these same records and marketed gun regulations to gun owners. The NRA would probably lobby to have their actions prohibited.

If the gun lobby believes that government, whether state or federal could not obtain similar lists, given its far greater reach, it is being naive. An autocratic government would have little difficulty compiling lists of owners from these sources, as well as from credit card records, easily obtained from financial institutions. It ought to be incumbent upon a democratic government to keep such lists to ensure that it citizens are safe from extreme gun owners.

Criminals Will Find a Way - If We Outlaw Guns Only Outlaws Will Have Guns

According to Rep. Mike Rogers (R-MI)[61],

> "Bad guys are going to get guns, they're going to get clips and they're going to do bad things."

The more difficult we make it for criminals to get guns, the less likely they are to have them and to use them. That is the whole idea behind gun restrictions. The Europeans and Japanese have managed to keep their gun deaths extremely low in comparison with the United States by controlling who has access to guns. If they cannot get them, they cannot use them. In addition, if only criminals had guns, law enforcement would know precisely who the criminals are.

Banning or restricting firearms raises the price of firearms, whether on the black market or the gray market, and makes them significantly more difficult to obtain. This is the precise intention of gun regulations. Fewer guns on the street ultimately result in fewer killings and injuries. Purchasing firearms on the black market can be a dangerous occupation considering the kinds of people involved in the trade. Only someone particularly desperate will take the chance of being robbed or shot merely to own a firearm.

The cost of purchasing a firearm on the black market can also be exorbitant. For an assault weapon like the Bushmaster used by Adam Lanza in his assault on the Sandy Hook Elementary School, the retail cost is between $1000 and $2000. The street cost could well be in the region of $5,000 to $10,000 for the same weapon[62]. Few criminals would want to pay as steep a price, or could afford to do so.

The point of comprehensive background checks and other laws is to make purchasing a firearm illegally as difficult as possible. In that way, fewer firearms would end up on the street. Not only that, but for the average citizen who has no experience of moving in criminal circles, knowing how and where to purchase an illicit firearm is close to impossible. Gun traffickers do not advertise themselves in the local newspaper. People with criminal records may also be prohibited from purchasing a firearm; buying one on the street risks not only his life, but comes with the risk of arrest and imprisonment for violating parole.

If fewer firearms were available on the legal market, fewer criminals would be able to procure firearms, whether through theft or through the gray or black markets. As a South African police chief pointed out, reducing the availability of firearms in that country was instrumental in reducing the firearm homicide rate. The answer to criminals obtaining firearms is to restrict the firearms that civilians can purchase, and the ammunition that they can retain at any one time. Restrictions on large capacity magazines, assault weapons, straw purchases, private sales and safe storage laws all help to keep guns out of the hands of prohibited persons. As the supply of firearms dries up, criminals will find it increasingly difficult to obtain or keep firearms, especially if firearms are confiscated from felons and other prohibited persons.

In order to claim that criminals will find a way, gun proponents must show how they might obtain those firearms, in order for society to close down those highways. No anti-gun-violence advocate ever claimed that it is feasible to prevent all gun violence, but we can go a long way towards reducing it, and that is what gun regulation proponents want. Gun proponents demand laws that prevent 100% of gun violence or massacres, and that is just not going to happen, certainly not given our current level of technology. There may come a time when technology will enable us to prevent all violent crime, but it is unlikely. Certainly allowing everyone to be as well armed as they please has not reduced gun violence to the levels of other nations that do have gun restrictions.

Criminals, or other prohibited persons may obtain firearms through theft or the illicit market, but most illicit firearms are sourced from friends or family members through straw sales, without background checks. These purchases account for close to 50% of trafficking investigations[63]. Thefts account for between 10% and 15% of crime guns[64], it takes too long for guns to filter to the street through theft for criminals to wait for those guns. Straw sales often happen when two or more people enter a gun store and the single authorized person purchases the firearms[65]. Most of the remaining crime guns are sourced from firearm licensees.

The single most common source for gun trafficking of illegal guns is corrupt gun dealers[66]. While most guns can be traced to a small number of dealers, a national telephone survey determined that half of gun dealers were willing to sell firearms under questionable circumstances, regardless of the end user. Dealers in the Midwest, South and West were more willing to sell under these conditions than those in the Northeast[67]. It is clear that a greater level of compliance needs to be imposed on dealers to prevent selling to questionable buyers. If gun dealers cannot trade honestly, the ATF should revoke their license to trade, as is currently done with cigarettes and alcohol.

When gun dealers become vulnerable to sting operations by law enforcement such as the ATF, lawsuits by city officials or bad publicity, they were far less likely to engage in illicit gun deals, and guns getting to the illicit market decrease significantly[68]. Increasing funding to ATF and allowing for monitoring of gun dealers would result in far fewer guns reaching the street. The gun lobby has systematically opposed any such legislation, which ensures the continued flow of guns to the streets.

Retaining records of background checks and firearms sold; cooperation with ATF gun trace requests; and mandatory reports of thefts or loss of firearms, would go a long way towards ensuring the safety of the public and a reduction in trafficking[69]. The restrictions placed on the ATF, who are only permitted to inspect gun dealers once a year and the lenient penalties for violating gun laws are instrumental in ensuring that gun trafficking continues[70].

If federal laws dealing with the retail purchase of firearms were extended to private sales and transfers, the flow of firearms to prohibited persons would fall. The recovery of crime guns found that as many as eight-five percent were recovered from someone other than the original purchaser[71]. Since the limitations in federal law permits increased trafficking of firearms, it is up to state and local officials to hold dealers accountable for gun transfers.

It is up to Congress to ensure that law enforcement agencies have the tools at their disposal to ensure compliance with the law, including firearm laws. By defunding agencies, or not providing sufficient funding, it is the fault of Congress that laws are not enforceable, as has been done by limiting the ability of the ATF to fight gun crimes.

Gun Trafficking

If gun dealers are held accountable for the firearms that they sell, fewer firearms are likely to end up on the illegal market. Given the eviscerating of the ATF's ability to inspect gun dealers on a regular basis, more firearms are sold illegally, and end up in the illegal market.

Gun trafficking is instrumental in moving firearms from the legal market to the gray and black markets. This is why treaties such as that proposed by the United Nations to restrict illegal weapons trafficking are so important. The gun lobby opposes any such legislation on Second Amendment grounds. Gun trafficking can and does allow guns to end up in the hands of criminals, drug gangs, terrorists, violent non-state actors, and repressive regimes, which is why the treaty is so important. The gun lobby prefers guns being available to the aforementioned groups than compromising on reasonable legislation and treaties.

Speculating that criminals may find other ways to obtain weapons as a defense against any gun limitation legislation is disingenuous. Many things are criminalized, drug trafficking, human trafficking, and wildlife trafficking, and they do still happen; that does not mean that we should legalize any of them. We need to find ways to prevent gun trafficking, not throw up our arms in surrender at the first sign of illegal activity.

Studies find that states with higher levels of gun ownership are linked to increased interstate gun trafficking. Regulation and oversight of gun dealers and regulation of private sales of handguns is likely to lead to lower levels of interstate gun trafficking[72].

In California, all firearm transfers must be routed through licensed retailers, which makes private sales illegal. Law enforcement is better able to solve crime and track illegal weapons by tracing the most recent purchaser. This enhances the ability of law enforcement to solve crime. In that state, 95% of people prohibited from gun ownership who committed gun crimes obtained these weapons privately[73].

Americans for Gun Safety reports that the 54,694 crime guns traced between 1996 and 2000 were purchased from 120 stores, accounting for 15% of traces during these years. Most of these stores were in 22 conservative states, including Indiana, Georgia and Virginia, with the exception being Illinois and Maryland[74]. 96 of these stores were still open in 2004, while some that have reopened after being shut down by the ATF had the same management as before.

Protecting Terrorists and Felons

Our pre-9/11 gun laws allow our enemies in the War on Terror to arm themselves right here in our own country **(Carolyn McCarthy)**

The absence of background checks at gun shows or for private transfers of firearms is a glaring deficiency in gun laws that encourages people with criminal, gang or terrorist sympathies to buy their weapons away from retailers. Whether terror groups like Al Qaeda have any meaningful presence in the U.S. is debatable, but people sympathetic to their cause or aspire to belong to the group, could feasibly use gun shows or Internet purchases to obtain assault weapons.

There is the very real danger that terror groups could stockpile deadly weapons and ammunition, and commit a dramatic atrocity in a public place like a sports stadium, shopping mall, tourist destination or other high profile setting. There is nothing stopping anyone on a terrorist watch list from purchasing assault rifles or pistols and ammunition freely. The massacre in Newtown could easily become a poster child for psychopathic groups set on maximizing civilian casualties using the unregulated availability of firearms.

Dangerous felons, recently released from prisons, are quickly and easily able to obtain weapons capable of destructive acts just as easily as are potential terrorists. In much the same vein, drug gangs who trade with gangs from Mexico, Colombia and other Central or South American nations are able to trade firearms for drugs.

Equally, drug gangs, who already have informal networks, could acquire arsenals of destructive weaponry to use against law enforcement or against other gangs. This is easily accomplished using straw purchases, gun shows or the Internet to obtain firearms and ammunition. Having gangs engaged in firefights is not only deadly to the gangs, but to any civilians caught in the crossfire. In some parts of the country, drive-by shootings are all too regular, with innocent civilians becoming unwitting victims.

By hindering background checks, the gun lobby is facilitating gang violence, the drug trade, gun ownership by felons and potentially arming the enemy. There is nothing in the Constitution that insists that we should arm society's enemies, and in fact there are portions of the Constitution that specifically speak about armed insurrection, which was the original intent of the Second Amendment.

Banning High-Capacity Magazines Won't Make Us Safer

High capacity magazines are not needed for self-defense, nor are they needed for hunting. The chances are that a home invasion is not going to involve more than one person. No-one needing to spray thirty bullets around their home should be in command of an assault weapon to begin with. The chance of stray bullets killing innocent bystanders is all too great given the fact that most homes are not made to withstand high-powered weapons.

A hunter who needs thirty bullets to kill an animal, should not be in control of any weapon. As it is, hunting causes untold suffering to animals when hunters miss their mark or hit an animal in the stomach or other part of the body without killing them.

High capacity magazines are used more often in mass shootings than are assault weapons, allowing shooters to kill and injure a greater number of people and hit a single person with a greater number of rounds, increasing the likelihood that the shooting will be fatal. The recent highly publicized mass shootings in Aurora, Colorado, Newtown, Connecticut and Tucson, Arizona all involved high capacity magazines.

Adam Lanza only reloaded his weapon four times using the standard 30 round magazines on his Bushmaster in Newtown, Connecticut. James Holmes used a drum magazine containing 100 rounds in shooting 70 people in 90 seconds in Aurora, Colorado.

Enforce the Laws Already on the Books

This is another red herring rolled out by the gun lobby whenever there is a push for greater gun regulation. The government cannot enforce laws on the books if those laws are ineffective at regulating people's aberrant behavior. If gun laws are not effective, we need to change those laws to reflect the realities faced by society. President Clinton wanted 1,100 more prosecutors at the end of his 8-year term,

500 more ATF agents, and $10m for smart gun research[75]. The gun lobby immediately responded that he should enforce the laws already on the books, without specifying which laws these might be. The gun lobby really needs to produce those laws it believes should be enforced before proposing this type of solution.

Given the current state of firearm laws, it is difficult to hold licensed or private sellers accountable if they sell firearms to prohibited persons. Private sellers do not have an obligation to determine whether those to whom they sell would pass a background check, or whether they are legally able to possess firearms. Laws prohibiting straw purchases or firearm trafficking are either poorly defined or non-existent[76].

Penalties for violating strengthened laws against gun trafficking ought to be increased to create a disincentive for illegally providing firearms to criminals or other prohibited persons. Without those disincentives, there is no reason for corrupt traders to obey the law, or to self-regulate. Instead of placing the burden on distributors and retailers, where it should be, to ensure that their sales are above board, the burden is on law enforcement agencies to enforce non-existent or weak federal or local laws.

Given that there are only about 300 laws governing firearms in the 50 states, as opposed to the 20,000 claimed by gun proponents including the gun lobby, law enforcement does not have the tools at its disposal to prevent gun crimes. The Tiahrt Amendment protects manufacturers and retailers from prosecution despite their knowingly selling firearms to criminals. In this environment, it is not feasible to successfully enforce non-existent laws.

An ATF investigation into NICS violations between 2002 and 2003, determined that of the 120,000 people denied permission to purchase a firearm, only 154 were prosecuted. The reason is that historically, prosecutions were *"unsuccessful in achieving convictions in many of these cases"*. US Attorneys are *"unwilling to expend their limited resources on prosecuting most NICS cases"*[77].

Why People Own Guns

Force and mind are opposites; morality ends where a gun begins (**Ayn Rand**)

Military dictatorship is born from the power of the gun, and so it undermines the concept of the rule of law and gives birth to a culture of might, a culture of weapons, violence and intolerance (**Benazir Bhutto**)

Some gun advocates claim that those who do not have guns are freeloaders on those who do, and that crime is reduced because more people have firearms. This is the only country in the developed world in which members of the public have to be concerned about others possessing firearms. No other nation in the developed world has this level of gun violence. Gun owners are not making us safer, they are making us far less safe. Not only that, but we have to pay the price of gun violence through our taxes.

The Illusion of Self-Defense

A common argument in favor of firearm possession is that carrying a firearm improves the safety of the carrier. This implies that the state is incapable of providing a secure environment for its citizens. If a singular reason for the state is to provide greater security to its citizens, this idea undercuts the existential reason for the state. An appeal to the evidence shows that access to firearms increases the insecurity of individuals within the state, and shows that a firearm is especially poor at providing defense for the individual. It also places those without firearms at a distinct disadvantage in a confrontation. If everyone were armed, it would only increase the likelihood that any confrontation would lead to severe injury or death. In confrontations without weapons, while injury is still feasible, it is far more difficult to cause death.

Firearms also provide the carrier with the illusion that they are able to use the firearm to deter an attack that is not life threatening, or even during situations that do not constitute an attack at all. Firearm possession can lead people to believe that they are in threatening situations when it is not the case, leading them to use firearms improperly.

It is also far too easy for a firearm owner to become aggressive without those around them because they have the belief that they are now immune from harm. This increases the risk to the population not similarly armed and decreases their security. The gun owner now becomes the individual personification of the authoritarian state, leading to intimidation and fear for those around them.

If self-defense with a firearm is rare in comparison with gun homicides, which is in fact the case, it is axiomatic that firearms are more likely to be used to murder and injure. Possession then is more likely to lead to criminal action than otherwise, which should lead society to reduce availability of and access to firearms. A society, such as the United States, which does not reduce firearm availability is increasing the risk to their citizens and is thus derelict in its duty towards society.

An analysis of the link between gun possession and gun assault determined that those who carry firearms were 4.46 times more likely to be shot than those who did not carry. Those who carried and had time to resist and counter were 5.45 times more likely to be shot than those not carrying. According to the authors of the study, this may be partially explained by the fact that[1],

> "A firearm falsely empowers its possessor to overreact, instigating and losing otherwise tractable conflicts with similarly armed persons...Individuals may increase their risk of gun assault by entering dangerous environments that they would otherwise have avoided. Alternatively, an individual may bring a gun to an otherwise gun-free conflict only to have that gun wrested away and turned on them."

In addition, the probability of a successful defensive gun use by a civilian is extremely low, which should lead us to conclude that the risks of carrying a firearm outweigh the risks of not carrying.

Studies also show that merely being in possession of a firearm makes people suspect that others also carry a weapon, which makes the possessor more likely to use the weapon than those not in possession of firearms[2]. Possession also allows gun possessors to incorrectly perceive neutral or otherwise harmless objects as firearms and to act accordingly.

Possession creates an unnecessary paranoia about others in society, especially regarding people of other races, particularly African-Americans. White gun owners are more likely to believe that an African-American is carrying a weapon than a person of another race. Men exposed to firearms exhibited higher testosterone levels and were three times more likely to engage in aggressive behavior than those not so primed.

What this shows is that gun possession creates delusions in the possessor that makes them more likely to believe that an incident is threatening, to increase their level of aggression, and to use a firearm. Situations in which a firearm should not or would not normally be used, lead to lethal or injurious results.

If part of the reason for owning a firearm is to make the owner less concerned about home invasion, but ownership alters the perception of the relative harm others might do; owning the weapon exacerbates rather than alleviates concerns about safety. Since comparatively few owners are actually at risk of accident or homicide in the home, the needless concern raised by owning firearms is an unnecessary risk factor to the owner. People may think that ownership makes them feel safer, but it really heightens their awareness of societal risks and fosters the belief that society is less safe than it actually is.

If guns are used in self-defense so seldom, as based on the NCVS survey and on the number of justifiable homicides each year, the central argument of the gun lobby, which is that guns are needed for self-defense, is fatally flawed. Considering the great number of deaths and injuries by firearm, firearms are used far more often to commit homicide or suicide than to save lives. Add to that the number of injuries requiring emergency treatment and the use of firearms to intimidate, coerce, assault and oppress, and it is clear that the possession of firearms should be severely curtailed.

Similarly, claims made by the gun lobby that brandishing firearms to prevent crimes save cities and municipalities large sums of money are fundamentally flawed. If self-defense use is as rare as it appears, there is no tangible benefit to crime prevention services. Firearm ownership may increase costs to law enforcement when incidents are reported and need investigation or for the large numbers of deaths and injuries by firearm.

Guns Are Seldom Used for Self Defense

Of the 29,618,300 victims of violent crimes between 2007 and 2011, only 235,700 instances of self-defense involved a firearm. It is unknown whether the firearm was fired in these instances and it may include off-duty law enforcement officers. Of the 84,495,500 victims of property crimes during the same period, firearms were used 103,000 times in self-defense[3]. Thus, a firearm was used 338,700 times in five years according to the NCVS, compared to 12.5 million claimed uses by the gun industry, and that is despite the almost 300 million firearms in private hands around the nation. In Detroit, shooting the burglar prevented only two of 1,000 burglaries.

Contrary to the belief of the pro-gun lobby that firearms are used 2.5 million times each year for self-defense, cases of justifiable homicide are almost non-existent. For those cases in which women kill men, the data show just how seldom firearms are used in self defense. In 2010, there were 3 cases in California, 1 in Georgia, 2 in Indiana, and so on. No state exceeded 10, with the highest number being Texas at five[4]. If firearms were being used for self-defense to the extent claimed, there would be tens of thousands of cases of justifiable homicide each year.

A 1998 study found that in comparison to the number of times a firearm was used in the home for self-defense, there were four unintentional shootings, seven criminal assaults or homicides and eleven suicides. Guns are 22 times more likely to be used in criminal assault, accidental death or injury, suicide or homicide than for self-defense.

Firearms Allow the Weak to Protect Themselves

Claims are sometimes made that firearms allow people otherwise unable to defend themselves to take action against a larger opponent. Yet, the people that own most firearms are the very people from whom the weak need protecting. People found at shooting ranges in control of extreme weapons are most likely to be men, many of whom appear to be those that civilized people would rather not meet in a dark alley. Firearms may be the great equalizer, but the elderly, the infirm, the mentally ill and children are least likely to be carrying firearms for protection. Women are far less likely than men to want to carry firearms for protection, yet they are more likely to need protecting from abusive intimate partners or other relatives. If firearms were used defensively, women would be more, not less likely to carry firearms; clearly this is not the case.

Justifiable Shootings Seldom Happen

In Minnesota, the decade between 2003 and 2013 saw five total instances of justifiable use of a firearm in self-defense[5]. Based on state demographics and the pro-gun lobby statistics, there ought to have been at least 43,000 instances of self-defense in Minnesota each year, or 430,000 for the decade. Even if only a small percentage of people actually reported using their firearm in self-defense, there should still have been thousands of reported self-defense uses. That there were not undermines the pro gun lobby statistic. Gun proponents argue that firearms do not have to be fired in order to be a deterrent, which may be true, but there are still no statistics proving unequivocally that firearms are used to prevent crime millions of times each year.

In Minnesota, firearm permit holders were convicted of 124 crimes involving firearms in the decade ending in 2013[6], as compared to five justifiable shootings, or 24.8 times as many gun crimes as lawful defensive uses over a decade. Gun proponents claim that many instances are not reported, which is unlikely, since people tend to contact law enforcement more often than not. Even in the extreme case that vastly more self-defense uses are not reported, it still does not comport with a ratio of five reported cases to 430,000 allegedly unreported cases over a decade.

In 2010, for every justifiable homicide, there were 17.9 gun homicides, and 31 firearm suicides. Firearms are used far more often to murder others or commit suicides than they are in fatal self-defense cases. While there are few freely available data to show the number of instances in which a firearm was used in non-fatal instances, it is unlikely to be substantially higher than NCVS data.

Gun Possession as a Deterrent

While gun proponents argue that the possession of firearms in the home is a deterrent to would-be home invaders, a would-be criminal, being of sound mind, would take precautions to guard against being confronted by an armed occupant. Typically, those intent on robbery will wait until occupants are not home, or if that is not possible, are otherwise occupied. If the residence is occupied, invaders will ensure that they are similarly armed to the occupant. Lastly, if arms are a deterrent, given the large numbers of firearms already in circulation, a prospective burglar must rationally assume that all occupants are armed, whether they are or not, and plan accordingly. This may make everyone less safe, since burglars are more likely to use lethal force if confronted during a home invasion. The firearm ownership of large numbers of people may thus increase the risks to those households that do not have firearms.

Given the heightened risk of confronting a burglar to save property, it is far more prudent to allow a burglar to take the property than to attempt to use a weapon to stop the burglary. The property certainly is not worth the added risk to life taken in a confrontation. An armed burglar may shoot first to mitigate the threat to his own life, or take the weapon away and use it on the owner. Additionally, as occupants of robbery targets become more well armed, intended criminals are likely to respond by improving their own armaments; an arms race, which no-one ultimately wins. It is far more sensible to allow law enforcement to do what they have been trained to do.

Self Defense or Excessive Force

A 2002 study of 297 defensive gun uses found that 27% may have been unnecessary or *"exceeded a defensive purpose"*[7]. Yet another study in 2004 determined that, among California teens, *"most reported gun uses were hostile interactions between armed adolescents."*[8]. In this study, 4% of adolescents reported being threatened with a firearm as against 0.3% using a firearm in self-defense; thus, adolescents were victimized 13 times more often. Self-defense with a firearm is therefore a rare occurrence among California youths. Additionally, many of the reported self-defense uses were during armed confrontations.

A 2000 study to "determine the relative incidence of gun victimization vs. self defense gun usage by civilians in the U.S" determined that far more people reported threats or intimidation with a gun than having used a gun to protect themselves[9].

There is also the open question of whether what people report as defensive gun use, such as brandishing a gun can be termed self-defense. In a social confrontation when tempers are roused, people may feel that they are invoking self-defense when pulling a firearm, but it is questionable whether their lives were truly at risk, or whether they are just intimidating others or threatening their lives. Without corroboration from neutral witnesses, the other parties to a confrontation may feel that they had as much right to self-defense as the gun owner, or that their actions did not constitute a threat to life or property.

The mere drawing of a weapon does not itself constitute self-defense unless there is a truly compelling threat of harm to life or limb. A simple altercation should be insufficient to warrant the threat of firearm use. The threat of firearm usage under similar circumstances could feasibly be seen as the aggressive use of a firearm, and not defensive. This is the problem with self-reporting of such incidents - there is often little evidence to corroborate allegations. If we are to claim millions of uses of firearms in self-defense, how many might credibly be classified as aggressive use of a firearm, which would be reported as seldom as self-defense uses. In any confrontational situation, do you count the use of a firearm as self-defense, taking the gun owners word, or as aggressive, taking the opponents' word?

Researchers such as John Lott, author of "*More Guns, Less Crime*", make the case that many instances of self-defense are not reported to law enforcement. If one party to an altercation feels that there is sufficient justification to draw a weapon, even if only to brandish that weapon, there ought to be sufficient justification to file charges against the other party. If there is not, there was insufficient justification to draw the weapon in the first instance. We as a society ought to resolve our differences through legal channels, not though vigilante justice, where an individual acts as judge, jury and executioner.

A simple argument or altercation should not be sufficient justification to sentence someone to death, even in the case of simple assault. To do so amply demonstrates depraved indifference to human life. An attempt should always be made, in a civilized society, to de-escalate a confrontation, even to the point of walking away, or "retreating". The very idea of not having to retreat is a primitive manifestation of excessive machismo, that all too often costs lives.

Populations at Least Risk Own Most Firearms

Paradoxically, older white men possess firearms in greater numbers than do other demographic groups, yet there is less risk of armed confrontation for white men, and especially older men, than for most other groups. The people most likely to be targeted are black men between 15 and 24, who die at a rate of 65.16 per 100,000, while white men die at a rate of 6.3. White men over 40 only die at a rate of two per 100,000. Whites, especially older white men have far less need for defensive firearms than do African Americans, and white women over 40 even less so, at a rate of 0.9. Younger males are affected far more than older men, the critical age group being between 15 and 24. Weapons for self-defense hypothetically should be possessed by those who are prohibited from using them, young black men under the age of 18.

Firearms purchased ostensibly for self-defense in the home are more likely to be used on the occupants of the home. Firearms are more likely to be used against women and children to intimidate, threaten, or assault than they are to be used in self-defense against an intruder. Firearms kept for self-defense in the home are 43 times more likely to kill someone known to the homeowner than to kill in self-defense[10].

Gun advocates contend that firearms can protect against rape and murder by strangers, and yet people close to home; friends, family members and lovers commit most instances of rape and murder. Instead of offering protection from attack by invaders, firearms in the home are more likely to be used during episodes of domestic violence. Women in a home with firearms are three times more likely to be killed by an intimate partner than are men[11]. A current or former intimate partner killed 40% of female homicide victims 15-50. Of those, 55% were killed by firearm.

Husbands or intimate acquaintances kill twice as many women as strangers using any method. Women living in a home with firearms are three times more likely to be killed in their homes than are women living in homes without firearms. Women killed in homes by a spouse, acquaintance or relative were 7 times more likely to live in homes with at least one firearm and 14 times more likely to have a history of domestic violence than women killed by a non intimate acquaintance[12]. Assaults with firearms are 12 times more likely to result in death than assaults using other means. Women who purchase firearms are 50% more likely to be killed by an intimate partner than are women who do not.

Gun proponents sometimes make the claim that visibility or knowledge of a firearm is sufficient to deter crime. Yet, studies show that visibility is enough to increase confrontations between people. The presence of firearms is enough to increase aggression in people; even pictures of firearms suffice to increase naturally aggressive tendencies.

Gun Lobby Paranoia Sells More Firearms

The gun lobby has created an unrealistic fear of crime and of home invasion to justify selling extreme weaponry to untrained citizens. The net result is an unwarranted rate of death and injury to cater for a low probability event. Ultimately in a country as safe as the United States, possession of a weapon for self-defense is not justified, and dangerous for all concerned. The real dangers we face are from the very guns that the firearm industry proposes we need for protection.

Over the past few centuries, crime and especially violent crime has fallen dramatically, due not to the ownership of more weapons, but to the fact that society has come to rely more on the use of the justice system and the courts to solve disputes rather than on extra-judicial self-defense. The gun lobby wants to reverse that centuries long decline and force individuals to rely on private firearm ownership for security rather than law enforcement. We should be relying more on the rule of law than the rule that might makes right.

It is quite possible that the introduction of Stand Your Ground laws coincided with the understanding that low levels of justifiable homicide argue against having firearms for self-defense. Legitimizing murder or manslaughter will have the effect of changing the ratios of justification in favor of the gun lobby, regardless of the moral implications of permitting extra-judicial killing. Justifiable homicide is currently a low frequency event; in 2010, fifteen states reported no justifiable homicides[13].

Risks of Ownership Outweigh the Benefits

In a society in which more than a third of people possess firearms, and there are 300 million privately owned firearms, there is no substantial advantage to being armed. The odds are, given that one in three people are armed, and that one in two men are armed, that both parties to a confrontation are armed. The singular result from drawing a weapon during an altercation is that the conflict escalates to the point that one or both parties will suffer a fatality. What being armed does do is place those who are not armed, or at least similarly armed at a distinct disadvantage; unable to defend themselves against those who are armed. If neither party were armed, the odds of a fatality drop significantly, thus, the fewer weapons in private hands, the less likely it is that an altercation ends in tragedy.

The available evidence indicates clearly that guns do not enhance safety, especially in the home and are more likely to increase risks to occupants. The available evidence thus refutes the claim that guns are necessary for self-defense. Not only do guns make the home less safe, they make society less safe for everyone. Most owners of handguns own them for self-protection, yet those guns actually make them less safe; thus, it is not rational to own a firearm at all. If on balance they are more likely to be used to harm a member of the household than to be used in self-defense against an attacker, the only logical choice to improve personal security is not to have a firearm in the home.

Guns and the 'Real Man'

Another favorite tactic of the pro-gun lobby is to portray the gun owner as a rugged individual, for whom gun ownership epitomizes masculine values, and a frontier, pioneering spirit. Non-gun owners are seen as, in one tolerant commentators words, *"effete liberal P*ssies"*.

A real man has no need of a gun to prove his manhood, he does it by taking responsibility for his spouse and children, by providing for them as best he can, or just as reasonably, living a life that does not involve the indiscriminate slaughter of animals he does not need for food, or for poisoning his environment. A man who wants to prove himself, if he really needs to, can climb a mountain, swim the English

Channel, sail around the Cape of Storms in a dinghy, or leap off a bridge with a bungee cord. Any buffoon with a finger can pull a trigger, it no more proves his manhood than does rape, assault or spousal abuse.

Guns and the Self-Reliant

The gun lobby focuses on firearms as instruments of self-reliance. There are many reasons that we live within an organized society, the least of which is that we rely on that society for safety and security. We do not live on the open frontier with a need to protect ourselves against armed marauders. We rely on our society having a force sufficiently well armed to defend the homeland from attack, a state militia to protect us from armed insurrection and law enforcement to protect us from those intent on criminal mischief.

Just as we rely on dentists to care for our teeth, mechanics to repair our vehicles and governments to maintain our roads, we cannot be expected to provide the means for our own defense. Civilized societies rely on organized, trained law enforcement to do that job for us. For instance, we cannot expect an elderly man or woman, who may have trouble hearing or seeing or with their mobility, to rely on personal self-defense measures to ensure their safety. They have a moral right to expect, and society a moral duty, to provide them with protection, not a society using armed, untrained vigilantes, but trained, official law enforcement.

Men, especially young men, commit most gun crimes and gun homicides. Encouraging young men to arm themselves only exacerbates the problem, rather as advertising fast cars to young men increases accident fatalities. Women are far more likely to be killed by men than are men by women. Considering the tone-deaf advertising campaign by the makers of the Bushmaster, which promises to "consider your man card reissued ", in the wake of the devastating massacre in Newtown using a Bushmaster, perhaps the testosterone charged environment of the gun industry needs to be toned down.

The implication of owning extreme firearms like the Bushmaster is that men feel empowered, and better equipped to instill fear in others. Especially in modernized societies like the United States, men have lost much of the traditional power they once had to dominate others, especially women and minorities who now have far more economic power than before. The ability to possess extreme weapons returns some of that lost power to men and gives them an artificially induced social status.

Projecting Power with Guns

The possession of a firearm promotes a combination of danger and control that is appealing to many men. It also promotes a false sense of bravado that all too often ends in tragedy for those around them. Firearms project a sense that the owner is a man of action and potential violence who cannot be controlled. Women too may be attracted to men who appear to project power through violence, and men who claim to protect their families from violent criminals. Add to that one mans promise to start shooting people if his guns were taken away and the gun industry's threat to take down the state, and men, especially white men appear to have convinced themselves that they are taking back power with their firearms.

The American gun ownership faction encourages the use of violence to resolve disputes instead of rational disputation and the judicial system, as witness the Stand Your Ground laws infesting many states. The firearm industry perpetuates the use of violence as a solution to society's travails rather than as an absolute last resort. The media encourages the glorification of violence, which is carried to its logical conclusion by the gun industry, with the notable distinction that a real firearm is fatal where the virtual or the movie version is not. The portrayal of gun-toting men as heroes in society only serves to reinforce this perception and encourage greater levels of violence in order to assume the mantle of superhero.

Mirroring the white male obsession with firearms, 56% of white males oppose stricter gun regulations. Only 10% of women own firearms, while 59% of women favor stricter gun regulation[14]. Most women oppose gun ownership to a large degree, while men claim they are protecting their women. Clearly, women do not agree that they are being protected and defended. Nearly 6 in 10 American gun owners are white men, with 74% of gun owners being male and 82% white. Just 6% of African Americans own guns.

The gun industry exploits the idea that a firearm will improve ones masculinity, enabling them to make huge profits from the white male sense of personal vulnerability and loss of power. The ability to carry a firearm anywhere he goes is really just an affirmation of his social vulnerability and inadequacy, a way to show that people cannot push him around as they do in every other sphere of life. With a firearm on his hips he can project braggadocio and bravado, secure in the knowledge that if someone challenges him, he can shoot first and use Stand Your Ground to ensure that he is not charged with homicide or manslaughter. It is either the ultimate form of extreme bullying, or a way to stop the bullies around him.

Guns are a God Given Right

And he shall judge among the nations, and shall rebuke many people: and they shall beat their swords into plowshares, and their spears into pruning hooks: nation shall not lift up sword against nation, neither shall they learn war any more.. (Isaiah 2:3-4).

"For all who draw the sword will die by the sword" (Matt. 26:52)

Quite possibly the most inane argument given by gun rights groups is that the Second Amendment is a God-given right. Wayne LaPierre had this to say about the right to armaments and self-defense,

> "They are God given freedoms. They belong to us in the United States of America as our birthright. No government gave them to us and no government can take them away."

The Constitution was not a document drawn up by God; men of great insight, but flawed people nonetheless, drew up the Constitution. People, societies, and communities together decide how to order their society, just as this one did and in so doing, produced a document filled with some wisdom, but also fatal flaws. The Second Amendment was poorly drafted and somewhat unclear in its intent, leaving the door open to the flagrant perversions of that intent as seen in the gun lobby. LaPierre cannot interpret the Constitution as an absolutist document; rather it is versatile and malleable enough that we can adapt it for use in a modern society.

People debase and exploit Scripture and other holy books to justify their own prejudices and ideologies, often with disregard to the intent of those works. It is no different when people like Wayne LaPierre and others use those texts, or a Constitution, to justify the possession of extreme weapons. As the verse from Isaiah intimates above, we should beat our guns into stop signs and our assault weapons into traffic lights where they would do some good for society. As a professed Christian, and I have no doubt he would profess to be such, LaPierre cannot just ignore the verse above and place his interpretation of the Constitution, above Scripture. Jesus did not need weapons, just as he had no need for wealth, instead he used the power of his words to persuade, not the power of the bullet. That, indeed, is the real power of the Christian philosophy; those who would use violent means to achieve their ends only succeed in perverting the religion.

The swords that Jesus often used in his pronouncements were mostly not physical swords, but metaphysical ones, the idea that the power of ideas has the ability to divide, to change minds and separate believers from non-believers. Much of what he taught was in the form of parable or metaphor, rather than explicit instruction. The swords mentioned in Luke 22:36, *"But now if you have a purse, take it, and also a bag; and if you don't have a sword, sell your cloak and buy one"* were used to convince the authorities that he was a brigand to fulfill the prophecy in Isaiah that he would be arrested and crucified. They were not intended for insurrection or defense against the state[15]. His power came through his philosophy rather than physical coercion, and any alternative interpretation was probably incorrect. The use of carefully selected verses, out of context, does not prove a biblical right to possess extreme firearms.

The idea persists on the right that we have a natural right to self-defense, but that has usually been the case. Everyone in this society has the right to defend his home and property; the issue is the means with which he may defend those things. Society has a right to lay down limits on those means; we may not surround our homes with landmines, tanks or machine guns. This is often because of the danger of using those things for offensive purposes, as well as the potential harm to non-aggressive neighbors. Likewise, society can regulate other extreme weapons, including assault weapons, LCM's, silencers and other items not necessary for protecting the home.

An appeal to arcane Scripture is not helpful in an age of assault rifles and other extreme weapons. Throughout history, people have used sacred texts to impose ideological idiosyncrasies on society, and extreme gun ownership in the United States is no different. No one is asking that people give up the right to self-defense, just that the safety of society is a consideration that may override individual demands.

Guns Don't Kill, People Kill

Yes, people pull the trigger -- but guns are the instruments of death. Gun control is necessary, and delay means more death and horror **(Eliot Spitzer)**

I keep hearing this [expletive] thing that guns don't kill people, but people kill people. If that's the case, why do we give people guns when they go to war? Why not just send the people? **(Ozzy Osbourne)**

This is a common argument used by gun extremists to justify ever-greater access to deadly weapons; guns do not kill people, people kill people. Like many slogans, it sounds compelling at first glance, but is no more cogent than any argument gun extremists make about armaments. The fact is that throughout history, people strived to create weapons of increasing lethality. The reason that they want these weapons is to kill greater numbers of opponents more efficiently.

We could use this argument going back to the Stone Age, in which we could say rocks don't kill people, or clubs, slingshots, atlatls, arrows, burning oil, muskets, cannon, matchlocks, flintlocks, or repeating rifles. The fact is that people develop increasingly lethal killing tools or machines because of the ease with which they can kill great numbers of people. Personal firearms are no different. They make it far easier for anyone to kill greater numbers of people than could be killed with all the weapons going back to the Stone Age combined. The more sophisticated weaponry becomes the more damage a single person can do with those weapons.

All those anachronistic weapons could also kill, just at a far less lethal rate than modern weapons. While it is possible for a mass killer to run around stabbing people to death, it is highly unlikely that he would get very far beyond a few people. The very fact that we can kill from a distance with a weapon that requires only occasional reloading shows that it is not guns that kill or people that kill large numbers of people, but people armed with lethal weapons that are able to kill large numbers of people. If we restrict access to those weapons, it becomes far more difficult for people intent on doing damage to harm too many people.

We do not allow civilians to purchase rocket launchers, tanks, missiles, chemical or biological weapons or atomic weapons. On their own, these things are just as inert as is a firearm. We do not allow people to own these things because of their use, which is to kill great numbers of people. People with missiles, atomic weapons or others kill, just as people with assault weapons kill far more efficiently than with alternative weapons. We produce a wide variety of tools to enhance our ability to do certain things.

We cannot build an apartment building, a motor vehicle or even a pair of shoes without using tools intended to make those jobs easier. Any tool that we use is ultimately an inanimate object that cannot do anything on its own, yet without that tool people cannot accomplish a wide range of tasks. The job of killing, in a macabre sense, is enhanced using increasingly efficient firearms. They are the tools that killers use to enhance their ability to take life, and they do that task in a most effective manner. If we restrict access to firearms, that occupation becomes redundant, just as the wheelwright became redundant when carts were no longer necessary.

In addition, if we know that certain people have a greater predisposition to use firearms to kill others, society has a right to demand that we keep weapons away from those people. That is why we want background checks to prohibit certain people from obtaining or using firearms. However, since we cannot tell with any degree of certainty which people are more likely to kill others with firearms, we need to restrict access to certain types of firearms, understand who owns firearms and prevent weapons from entering the public space. We should not have to trust in people's better nature.

Fascination with the Second Amendment

Perhaps people should be fascinated with the entire Constitution, not just a single amendment, and not a particularly well framed one at that. There are four amendments that secure the right to vote, those that guarantee the right to privacy, or the right to the religion of your choice, or to speak your mind regardless of who it is said to. To hear gun rights advocates speak, one would think that there was only a single sentence in the Constitution. The entire Constitution, not just the amendments, is what guarantees our freedom, our rights, not the Second Amendment, which has more to do with right of the states to lawfully constitute a militia than it does with any individual right to bear arms.

Having a civilian population possessing arms does nothing to ensure freedom, and everything to take unnecessary lives every year. There was no freedom for those killed; no rights, no liberties, just death. Other nations without the Second Amendment have fewer gun deaths, by which measure they are freer than are we, for I would rather have no guns and my life, than a gun and a mortuary slab as home.

Firearms as a Hobby

There is no reason that hobbyists cannot build parts for their guns at home. They can then take those parts down to the range and fit those parts to their weapons if they so desire. People who modify their weapons at home may end up with a weapon that is military grade or close to it, that improves the efficiency of their weapon to the point that it creates a public menace. The public ought to be able to regulate that activity.

Guns are not hobbies, they are machines of destruction, intended to kill. Creative people can indulge in hundreds of art forms that do not produce destructive works. There are few other hobbies as destructive to life as the firearm. Those who enjoy tinkering with machinery could convert the millions of vehicles on Earth to safer forms of fuel, which would do some good for the planet. Surely, some less destructive occupation might engage their minds.

Some gun proponents claim that no other hobby is subject to the kinds of restrictions demanded by gun regulation advocates. Scuba diving, knitting, non-gun sport or painting are welcomed around the world and generally not restricted. The obvious difference is that none of those hobbies is intended to harm, injure or kill either humans or animals. Scuba diving may be severely restricted depending on whether an area of the coast is considered endangered, or part of a national park.

The entire Galapagos Island chain is an ecological sensitive area that is severely circumscribed by the Ecuadorian government. Parts of the Great Barrier Reef are strongly regulated. Hobbies that pose a threat to life may be similarly regulated. People are generally not permitted to scale tall buildings, or to use skateboards or bicycles on the Golden Gate Bridge. There may be a great many regulations on hobbies, such as the inability to drive vehicles intended for motor sports on public highways.

When our hobbies or other activities are generally harmful, or pose a risk to others, it is incumbent upon society to regulate them and ensure that innocent bystanders are not harmed.

Gun proponents claim that there are no special interests wanting to regulate other hobbies, but that claim is untrue. There are groups concerned about the environment and overcrowding in resort areas that do want to limit public access to sensitive areas. People are concerned about runners or cyclists and want special areas created for them away from motorists, just as many people feel that firearms belong on gun ranges and not on the street.

The Second Amendment Makes People Feel Safe

The Second Amendment as it is currently implemented does not make me feel safe at all. As gun regulations have been relaxed, I feel ever more insecure, never knowing whether my neighbor is armed with forty weapons and substantial quantities of ammunition, never knowing whether I will go for a walk early one morning and end up shot as an intruder, as Trayvon Martin was by George Zimmerman. People should not have to live in fear of their neighbors, of being involved in a road rage incident in which a gun is pulled, of being shot getting the family garbage from the street.

People should have as much right to feel safe in their homes, communities, shopping malls or restaurants as the gun owner does. If people have to be concerned about gun owners walking into those public spaces fully armed, their right to enjoy being in public is in jeopardy. If people no longer feel safe in public, it restricts their free movement, their right to assemble and not worry about the armed gun owner at the next table. Many people feel intimidated when armed gun owners enter a public space. They have no way of knowing that these owners can be trusted, that they wont become aggressive, or drunk, and use those weapons. If gun owners were respectful of others, they would enjoy their weapons where non-gun owners do not spend their time, on gun ranges or clubs.

While the Second Amendment may make some gun owners feel safer, non-owners do not feel safer. All rights must be balanced with the need for safety and security and respect for the rights of others. Just as the First Amendment does not extend the right to impose images of pornography or graphic and gratuitous violence on others, nor does the Second extend the right to impose extreme weapons on society. All our rights are regulated to some degree, whether it is the right to drive, but not speed, the right to drink, but not before driving, the right to smoke, just not in restaurants or public spaces, gun advocates must realize that society can and must be regulated to account for the rights of others.

Firearms Guarantee Liberty

Gun advocates who believe that firearms guarantee liberty, or are an expression of liberty have no understanding of the victimization, the depravity, the slaughter of innocents around the world by armed men. Every politically treacherous hot spot around the globe is saturated with firearms and young men who use those weapons to intimidate, oppress, control, assault, rape, torture and kill. These are not expressions of freedom; they are pits of depravity where the vulnerable are preyed upon by those with arms.

In the inner cities, and poverty-stricken towns of this nation, guns are used to intimidate, to establish hegemony over others, to kill rivals, to defend against other school students because they have no choice. For children that feel compelled to carry firearms into classrooms because of the ever-present threat of gun violence, there is no freedom.

Firearms do not protect us from violence or tyrannical government; they do not guarantee our freedoms. Democratic institutions and respect for those institutions guarantee our freedoms. When we feel that we are free to speak our minds, to argue, to take our disputes to courts that work for us, when we are able to vote freely without governmental obstacles, when we are able to marry whomever we please, live wherever we please, educate ourselves and enjoy health, then we are free. Owning a firearm does none of that for us, and only increases fear and delusion.

The great mark of this nation is not the ability to own a firearm, it is a commitment to government that ensures and guarantees our liberties. True liberty is the absence of fear, the absence of violence, hunger and disease, and the understanding that anyone is able to succeed because government institutions guarantee that ability. No one that has to impose his liberty through the barrel of a gun is free, and neither is the person on the wrong end of that weapon.

It is odd that those who demand their liberty to own firearms do not similarly demand the right of minority groups to vote freely, that they feel the need to gerrymander districts, depriving people of the right to vote. They impose restrictions on voting rights, despite the fact that four Amendments guarantee that right. Nowhere in the Constitutions does it say that voting requires identification, yet the gun owning states impose that requirement on others.

The freedom demanded by gun owners is the freedom to impose their guns on others, to take the rights of others away through the implicit threat of force. The underlying idea is that they should have rights, but no one else can exercise their rights. Gun ownership is the ultimate tyranny.

Protecting the Family

We live in sophisticated, modern societies, with law enforcement officers who are trained in the art and science of protecting the community. We should not leave that up to individuals, nor should we have to. Any society that cannot protect its own from harm is no society in which to live. We can understand that you cannot stop all crime, but with the correct community attitudes, with a respect for law and order, we do not need to protect ourselves.

I have spent a lifetime in two violent countries, South Africa and the United States, and with a brief detour from sanity, have never felt the need to be armed. I expect that the society be sufficiently well defended by law enforcement that it is unnecessary to arm oneself.

People who say that they need an assault weapon to protect their families are living in a deluded world, a world of conspiracy and intrigue, of artifice and collusion. Their world is one in which no one trusts anyone else, where every neighbor, every stranger, anyone different is suspicious. They should try living in the Central African Republic, Rwanda, Mali or Afghanistan, where weapons are used to terrorize the people, as it is becoming here with arms being allowed wherever one goes.

It is the case in this country that people living in households with armaments are many times more likely to die from homicide than people living in households without deadly weapons. One cannot accept that the gun owner is truly protecting his family.

We do not for the most part, live out on the open prairie in the 1830's where there are numerous threats to life, and little or no law and order. We no longer have a duty to defend our homes from intruders. That duty has been outsourced to organized law enforcement, on which we rely. It is only in those communities that have chosen to dramatically cut budgets to save money where law enforcement is experiencing a reduction in numbers. In civilized societies, communities pool their resources to provide for the common defense. Even in Roman, or Medieval times, this was common. The local castle or fort was a refuge for the local people from marauding bands and it was stocked using taxes from the surrounding areas.

The very idea that we should all be armed, locked and loaded, waiting for the barbarians is an anachronism from the Dark Ages, not the greatest civilization known to man. The problem with using a weapon to defend a home is that it becomes too easy to see any intrusion as a threat to life and limb and use deadly force to prevent that threat. A young man hiding on a porch from the police is not a clear and present danger to the occupant of the home. That is the purpose of law enforcement. We should not be expected to police our homes or neighborhoods. People mostly do not have the skills to do this successfully.

Many people who are very young, very old, infirm, sick, incapacitated, or blind, or have no knowledge of firearms or desire to own them. We cannot just leave them to the depravations of those with criminal minds. We should cater for those who do not have the means, need or desire for personal weapons. There are many cultures around the world that have large, vulnerable populations and no effective law enforcement, filled with armed men, and they are not very pleasant places to live. We do not really want this country to be the same; we must get together as communities and establish laws to govern the use of force and the prevention of that force.

There are times when you do not have your weapon with you, in the shower, in bed, watching TV, cooking a meal. You are unlikely to carry your weapon at those times. Those with criminal intent will wait until you are in a disadvantaged position before preying on you. You cannot imagine that they are going to make it easy for you, by waiting until you are ready to fetch your weapon, before they enter your home. Truly, life is not a movie, and perhaps you have been watching too many. Life is far messier.

There is also the issue of the right of non-gun owners to protect their families. The fact is that the more guns are on the street, the more difficult it is to ensure that their families are safe from gun owners. The more legal guns there are, the more guns are stolen and end up in the wrong hands, which places those families at risk.

While you may want to have the right to protect your family and determine how that should be done, non-gun owners should have the right to determine how they want their families protected from people who own guns, whether they are legally owned or not. Perhaps they want to live in a society in which there are no guns, and if there are, that those guns are properly secure, licensed and legal, and that their owners are properly trained, and have no criminal background. They want to know when they move into a neighborhood that there are no gun owners, or if there are, that they are in fact responsible. The only feasible way to do that is to regulate the possession, licensing, usage and transference of firearms.

Weapons Are Part of History or Tradition

Unfortunately, this is true, and throughout that history, armaments have been used to intimidate, oppress, torture, assault, maim and massacre large numbers of people. The first implements used by people as weapons were crude and inefficient killing machines, so man got to work with his infinite intellect to develop more effective killing devices. The personal handgun is one of the most reliable, potent and capable killing machines known to man.

If your traditions are the proximate cause of the 30,000 people cut down by guns each year, it is time to change your traditions. If you go back far enough, most of our ancestors were cannibals, tortured people for their religious beliefs, or drowned witches. We do not do those things any more because we consider ourselves civilized; we do not need guns as part of our civilized culture.

If one needs to collect weapons because of their history, the firing mechanism can be removed to make them inoperable, and people can collect away. There are so many things a person could feasibly collect, with far more history attached; it is unnecessary to collect firearms in particular. People collect things from bottle tops to car tires, from ancient jewelry to paintings. Something else must sate the desire for hoarding other than a mechanical killing device.

People say that the assault weapon is as much a part of the history of this country as is the musket, the rifles carried in the trenches of Flanders Field, or any other weapon held by a soldier. They claim that to hold one in your hands and take it to a range to fire is a feeling that many do not appreciate. There is nothing to prevent them from keeping such a weapon at a gun range under lock and key and firing it there. There is just no reason to keep it at home. If someone wants to keep the weapon at home, remove the firing mechanism and display it on the wall. Either way, we do not need civilians in possession of destructive weapons.

When our traditions are found to be destructive, whether towards others, or our environment, we change those traditions and replace them with sensible conventions. Mans natural abilities allow us to improve our surroundings, the way we approach life; we realize that killing solves nothing, so civilized people find ways to stop killing. Banning or limiting firearms helps us accomplish just that. This is why Western Europeans have lived in almost total peace since the end of the Second World War.

Traditions like hunting are destroying our natural heritage for everyone, not just for those communities that have a tradition of hunting. Traditions that are transplanted from a rural setting to an urban one can cause the deaths of a great many people. This demonstrable lack of respect for a peaceful society by the gun lobby costs lives.

Urban areas and cities have a tradition in American history of restricting gun ownership, but the continuing push by gun proponents to prohibit sensible gun regulations is a violation of that tradition. The Southern states especially want to force firearms on urban areas that already have high rates of gun crime, threatening to make them worse. Traditions work both ways, and the rights of the city dweller must be weighed against those of rural areas.

Weapons are Cool

Many things on our planet are cool and do not destroy life. Those that do destroy life, we as a society regulate, and have a right to regulate, from Sarin gas to biological weapons. Cars are cool, a lot more so than firearms, but we still have strict regulations about what we allow on our roads, and the speeds at which they may be driven. For those people that have a desire to drive a vehicle at breakneck speed, we provide speedways and other racing venues. This keeps dangerous vehicles off the public roads and allows people to enjoy the highways without a severe threat to their lives.

Perhaps those who find weapons of mass destruction cool should try finding another image, one more suitable to a civilized society. The need to fit in to a group filled with killers is not something to which one ought to aspire. There are plenty of groups like that around the world, and none of them are in particularly hospitable parts of the world, certainly for the local population, who are generally intimidated, hunted and killed because they support or oppose some political, religious, racial or other arbitrary affiliation.

There was a time when smoking cigarettes was seen as cool, until people were forced to understand that tobacco kills people. Once that realization was imprinted on people, it became less glamorous to smoke, and smoking disappeared from movies, offices, and buses and anywhere in public. It will only be when people realize that guns are used to kill far too many people far too easily that society will regulate firearms. A dead body lying in a street riddled with bullets is not cool; the image of a women brutalized by a gun wielding husband is not cool; the image of twenty slaughtered children in a Connecticut school is not cool; the thought of a dead teen who went out for skittles and iced tea is not cool. Guns are not cool; they are used to injure and to kill.

Hollywood Glorifies Weapons

The idea that people own weapons because Hollywood glorifies them is just untrue. Many people, myself included, watch Hollywood movies, sometimes extremely violent movies and those movies in no way have any influence over my buying or using a firearm, or perpetrating any form of violence against others. Quite the contrary, as movies have become more graphic and violence grows in intensity, I am somewhat less likely to purchase a firearm. Having seen the mass destruction that might feasibly be wrought with these destructive devices, my intolerance towards weapons has become stronger than it has ever been.

People who buy into the G.I. Joe image of firearms should really understand that these are movies, not real life, that in civilized societies, we do not need to arm ourselves with destructive devices. Considering that movies and TV series have become more graphic and violent over time, the percentage of households in the United States having guns has dropped over time from around 50% in 1973 to around 30% in 2010. During the Rambo era, there were more households with guns than there are today. Yet, Rambo or The Godfather movies are considered relatively tame today.

All around the world, people watch the same movies as we do here in the United States, yet gun violence is declining as gun regulations are strengthened. Only in the United States do conservatives insist on proliferating access to deadly weaponry, while the people experience increasing gun violence.

The areas of the country in which there are more guns are always areas with higher levels of poverty, more religion, less education and less tolerance of other races, creeds, religions, nationalities or gender. It has little to do with Hollywood and much to do with tolerance of others. The John Wayne, Clint Eastwood Hollywood style protagonist may influence some people, but most people see this as an act, a story, with little basis in reality.

Wayne LaPierre, scion of the gun lobby had this to say about Hollywood movies[16],

> "We have blood soaked films out there like 'American Psycho' and 'Natural Born Killers'. They're aired like propaganda loops on 'Splatterdays' and ever single day ... Isn't fantasizing about killing people as a way to get your kicks really the filthiest form of pornography?"

In the National Firearms Museum at the NRA national headquarters, guns from some of the most violent movies Hollywood has made are clearly displayed. From "Heartbreak Ridge" and "The Wild Bunch" to "We Were Soldiers", "Die Hard" and "No Country for Old Men", none of these movies is a gentle romance[17]. The museum also highlights "Pulp Fiction", notably one of the most violent movies ever to come out of Hollywood. The NRA and the gun industry entice people to use real weapons to fantasize about killing others, and many of them use those weapons to take the lives of the nations wildlife. Pornographic, indeed!

The NRA museum also featured a production called "Hollywood Guns", which according to their website is "a firsthand glimpse of some of the most famous firearms on the silver screen over the last 70 years". The NRA claims that Hollywood is at fault, yet they glorify Hollywood history.

Reasonable Entertainers Oppose Firearms

Hollywood celebrities like Jessica Alba, Jennifer Garner, Cameron Diaz and others produced a campaign to demand an end to gun violence. Conservatives, who claim that Hollywood is hypocritical since they produce violent movies, roundly criticized the actors. Most, if not all of these actors act in movies in which there is very little violence, if any. Jamie Foxx, who also participated, does indeed make violent movies. Conservatives should realize that actors are at the mercy of producers, directors, writers and the public. Without public demand for violent movies, actors would not work on those projects. Hollywood is not a monolith, it contains as varied a population and variety of movie genres as anywhere else in the U.S. Some movies are violent and some are not, some producers make violent movies and some do not.

Conservative Actors Promote Firearms

I have a very strict gun control policy: if there's a gun around, I want to be in control of it. **(Clint Eastwood)**

Republicans tend to glorify firearms, and yet criticize Hollywood for purportedly doing the same. Yet, ironically, many of the actors that star in violent movies are Republicans or support Republican candidates for office. The obvious candidates are people like Arnold Schwarzenegger, famous for the unremittingly brutal "Conan", "Predator" and "Terminator" movies. Sylvester Stallone is renowned for the "Rambo" series and not a few violent cop movies, as well as "The Specialist", "Assassins", "Demolition Man" and other gratuitously graphic and violent films.

Chuck Norris, another ultra-conservative, made famous the "Walker, Texas Ranger" series that was at one time classified as the most violent series on TV. Mel Gibson starred in such sensitive classics as "Mad Max" and produced the ultra-violent "Passion of the Christ". Joe Pesci is one of the most bloodthirsty men in Hollywood movies, including such gems as "Goodfellas" and "Casino", both brimming with unwarranted cruelty. Bruce Willis movies are almost invariably violent and filled with firearms and explosions. Jerry

Bruckheimer produces some of the most violent series on the small screen and many violent movies including "Armageddon", "Pearl Harbor" and "Con Air". It is easy to wonder whether those attracted to violent action movies are more likely to be Republican than Democratic, both actors and producers.

What is more disturbing is that the NRA encourages people to actually own and use weapons portrayed in these movies, by taking them to firing ranges and on hunting expeditions. The organization glamorizes the ownership of assault weapons. Given the gratuitous violence displayed in movies and increasingly in real massacres on our streets and in our schools, one would imagine that a sane person would have nothing to do with these extreme weapons. The fact is that the NRA and the American gun industry glorify extreme firearms.

A contrast between many Hollywood TV series and the Canadian TV series "Flashpoint" demonstrates the difference in cultural norms between the U.S. and Canada. In "Flashpoint", the protagonists are members of a squad tasked with dealing with crimes, often gun crimes, and, just as in the U.S., carry extreme weapons. However, the Canadian production attempts to resolve problems by talking the antagonist down from committing a violent act and will do anything possible to ensure that they do not use their firearms. When they do kill, it is because they have absolutely no other choice, and they actually show remorse for their actions, often for many episodes following the killing.

In contrast, American productions resort to killing as a first resort, negotiation is seldom used, and the protagonists almost never show remorse for their killings, which they see as routine. The American productions are a reflection of the local gun culture and they cater to the violence in that culture. In Canada, gun violence is far less of a problem and they attempt to resolve issues rationally rather than with firearms.

There is at least the possibility that people who are more predisposed to purchase extreme weapons, or any firearms, are more likely to watch violent movies than those who do not purchase weapons. Movies made specifically for women, who are less likely to purchase firearms, are less likely to contain scenes with firearms, or at the very least, less likely to use them. For those who both purchase firearms and watch violent movies, their view of violence is tempered by what they watch, that is, they believe the world is a violent place because it is portrayed that way in the movies they watch. Believing that the world is a violent place, they buy firearms to combat that violence, which naturally leads to a more violent world; a violent feedback loop. People with a nuanced view of the world are more likely to watch a wide variety of entertainment, leading to a more realistic perspective of the world around them.

The fault for gun violence must be laid firmly at the feet of the gun industry, which forces extreme firearms on the population to increase their profits, regardless of the resulting death toll. Hollywood only produces movies that reflect that gun culture; they do not create it. It is hypocritical for the gun industry, whose products produce tens of thousands of deaths each year, to blame Hollywood for gun violence, since Hollywood, unlike the tobacco, alcohol and firearm industries do not produce products that cause death.

Gun Sales Improve the Economy

This is one of the more offensive arguments made for purchasing a firearm. Despite the tens of thousands of people killed and many more injured each year, the purchaser does not appear to comprehend the harm that his purchase has on society. Tobacco sales may help the economy, but also cost the economy billions of dollars to treat the resulting cases of cancer, emphysema, heart disease and stroke.

Likewise, the costs to the economy of combating ongoing gun violence more than offsets any temporary fillip to the economy by the gun industry. The lifetime medical costs and other costs to society in terms of lost productivity, depression and quality of life due to gun shot injury more than offsets the economic gain. We could argue that going to war is a stimulus to the economy, since war machinery has to be supplied, troops must be kept fed and the thousands of occupations required to keep the economy on a war footing also assist the economy. We must then consider the loss of life, and the destruction of homes and public infrastructure in target nations. The marginal boost to growth in no way justifies the death and injury incurred by free firearm availability.

Assault Weapons

Semi-automatics have only two purposes. One is so owners can take them to the shooting range once in a while, yell yeehaw, and get all horny at the rapid fire and the burning vapor spurting from the end of the barrel. Their other use -- their only other use -- is to kill people (Stephen King, Guns)

There is no justification for any civilian to own an assault weapon. While there are many reasons given, none hold water when closely scrutinized. Having an assault weapon and using it in a public place is the equivalent of driving a modified speedway vehicle down a public highway at a hundred and fifty miles per hour. It may feel cool, but it endangers the lives of other people and that is why we regulate that activity. Not allowing people to regulate guns is like allowing anyone to do as they please on a public highway, which costs peoples lives.

In the Aurora Theater, Colorado, the killer used, among other weapons, an AR-15 assault weapon. In the Connecticut school shooting in the Sandy Hook Elementary School, Adam Lanza used a Bushmaster AR-15 assault rifle to dismember twenty-six people. Jared Loughner, the man who shot Rep. Gabrielle Giffords and killed six others including a young 9-year old girl, used a high-capacity magazine. Seung-Hui Cho killed 32 people in Virginia Tech using high capacity magazines.

Andrew Arulanandam, NRA spokesman had this to say about Sen. Dianne Feinstein's push for an assault weapons ban,

> "In spite of what Senator Feinstein is trying to spin and put the blame on the NRA, the real reason that there is lack of support for these bans is because we had a 10 year period where these bans were the law of the land and during that 10-year period numerous studies were conducted that found these bans were ineffective at reducing crime."

In reply, Sen. Feinstein had this to say[1],

> "It had begun to do what we wanted it to do, which is to drive down the number of these guns over time. The NRA has their statistics, I have mine."

Subsequent to the introduction of the assault weapons ban in 1994, gun homicides fell dramatically until 1999, when they stabilized and started to rise. Since 2000, total gun deaths have risen, and since the expiration of the assault weapons ban have risen still further. As with all restrictions on firearms and ammunition, it takes some time for the supply of firearms to affect homicides and crime rates. Far from the ban having no effect, the ban appeared to have a powerful effect on reducing crime. There is no doubt that the current rise in homicide deaths is directly related to the gun lobby assault on the rights of the non-gun-owning public.

What is disturbing about the assault weapon market is that the gun industry specifically markets these weapons as military derivatives, appealing to people who glorify combat, or those who resent central government. The only real distinction between military assault weapons and civilian weapons is that military weapons have automatic fire enabled.

Assault Rifles

Assault weapons are semi-automatic firearms designed with military features allowing for rapid and accurate spray firing. Spray firing is the ability to move the weapon side to side, using a pistol grip or other device to prevent being burned. These weapons are not sporting weapons; they are designed solely to kill human beings quickly and efficiently[2]. Their characteristics include; detachable magazines, forward handgrips, barrel shrouds with magazine in front of the trigger, thumbhole stocks, folding or telescoping stocks and muzzle brakes or compensators.

Civilian Semi-Automatics Are Not Assault Rifles

I once had an on-line spat with someone who gave me an extended lecture on the difference between semi-automatic rifles and military assault rifles. As we argued about rate of fire and various other irrelevancies, I realized that we were working at cross-purposes. The fact that a civilian AR-15, which, for want of a better term is a semi-automatic assault rifle, can only fire up to 60 rounds per minute, depending on how fast the gunman can depress the trigger, whereas an automatic assault rifle like the M4A1 carbine can fire hundreds of rounds a minute, really is not the point.

When one person, wielding any weapon at all, but in the case of Newtown, a semi-automatic assault rifle, can enter a school, and in the course of about five minutes, kill twenty children and their six brave teachers, we should be banning those weapons. To those children and their wonderful teachers, those weapons were assault weapons, for that is what they did, they were used to assault the school and kill too many people, far too quickly and efficiently. The children were not having a pedantic debate concerning the rate of fire or relative lethality of this weapon; they were losing their lives in a firearm obsessive society. Civilians should not be able to attack any public or private place and kill so many so quickly.

People do not need these weapons for self-defense; they are not going to be assaulted by hordes of attackers, and if they were, those attackers would likely be similarly armed. We need to get the paranoia out of the public square and into psychiatric institutions where it belongs. We should take highly destructive weapons from civilians and give them to those tasked to protect us. That means law enforcement during peacetime operations and the military during war, and for no other purpose, at no other time.

Whether a firearm can fire a single bullet at a time is not the issue. It is how many projectiles can be released without reloading, how accurate the weapon is, how reliable it is, how easy it is to operate and whether it can be fired more swiftly than other weapons. The characteristics of assault-style weapons, like barrel shrouds and detachable magazines make for effective killing performance, and as such, they should be banned. Semi-automatic handguns are similarly more efficient weapons, raising the potential death rate over revolvers and other weapons.

Assault rifle expert C.J.Chivers puts it succinctly[3],

"Assault rifles ... were conjured to form solely for the task of allowing men to efficiently kill other men because they are smaller, lighter in weight, more tactically versatile and require a lighter per-man effective ammunition load than the infantry rifle that preceded them."

It does not matter that they are not automatic weapons or machine guns, what matters is that twenty children and six great teachers were killed in less than five minutes in the Newtown massacre. That this does not bother some gun owners displays a disturbing lack of empathy and an unwillingness to sacrifice anything for the greater good, even for their own children who may be victimized during a massacre.

What also matters is whether and how easily these weapons might be converted into fully automatic weapons. When small modifications produce a far more deadly weapon, the civilian version ought to be banned. When weapons possess a large number of military style features, they ought to be seen as close to military weapons. Many experts agree that automatic fire is not particularly accurate, while semi-automatic fire can be extremely accurate, especially given the physical attributes of assault weapons.

What is of great concern is the ease with which an assault-style weapon can be converted to close to automatic fire. An after-sales component that can easily modify an AK-47 or AR-15 civilian assault rifle, the slide fire stock is freely available. This addition enables accurate and controlled rapid firing, mimicking the operation of an automatic weapon. Yet, this modification does not violate the National Firearms Act. This is precisely why assault style weapons should be banned, given their potentially high rate of fire, accuracy and efficiency.

The Number of People Killed with Automatic Weapons is Small

The argument that we should be able to possess semi-automatic weapons is disturbing at best. The very idea that there is an acceptable loss to justify the possession of firearms is disgraceful. That any society would sacrifice people merely to allow possession of weapons of great destructive power goes against the grain of a lawful and peaceful society. We should do whatever we can to ensure that not one person dies unnecessarily, whether from firearms or from anything else.

In most areas of life, civil societies attempt to mitigate death. We expend vast amounts on trying to cure deadly diseases like cancer, heart disease and diabetes. We regulate motor vehicles and hold aircraft manufacturers to an inordinately high standard, despite the reality that few people die from aircraft disasters. It is only when dealing with gun deaths that the gun lobby and the Republican Party routinely and absolutely refuse to even discuss ways to reduce the high rate of death.

We in the United States consider our inordinately high rate of gun deaths to be a normal part of gun ownership, and that victims are forced to surrender their lives to ensure complete access to all firearms. Other nations have a differing perspective, and it shows in the dramatically smaller rate of deaths in those countries. The annual homicide death rate from long guns alone in the U.S. in 2011 was 0.22 per 100,000[4]. The total gun death rate from all causes and all kinds of firearms in the United Kingdom was 0.23 per 100,000 in 2011[5]. Thus, rifle and assault weapon homicides alone kill people at almost the same rate in the U.S. as do all people killed by all methods in the U.K. The total firearm homicide rate in Germany was 0.2 in 2010, less than the long gun rate in the U.S., and similar to the rate in France, at 0.22.

Even a small percentage decline in the total number of homicides countrywide can amount to a significant number of people. One estimate put the reduction in gun crimes involving assault weapons from 5% to 2% of the total[6]. Given the relative rarity of assault weapons, this translated to around a 1% decline in homicides with assault weapons. That still amounts to 110 fewer murders a year. Americans need to ask whether owning assault weapons is worth the price; 110 people per year, or more than 1,000 over a decade.

While the talk of assault weapons generally revolves around the perception of military-style assault rifles, there is also the use of assault pistols. The use of small, easily concealed semi-automatic pistols causes many more deaths than assault rifles. These weapons use extended magazines containing up to thirty rounds and can be fired as fast as anyone can depress the trigger. Bans on weapons such as the Tec-9 handgun, a favorite of drug gangs ought to be considered along with the bans on assault-style rifles.

Research has determined that assault weapons, whether pistols or rifles, are used disproportionately in murders with multiple victims, multiple wounds per victim and with police officers as victims[7]. Of the 211 police officers killed in the line of duty between 1998 and 2001, 20% of cases involved an assault weapon[8]. By this measure, assault weapons are a greater threat to law enforcement officers than they are to other civilians. There is no reason that law enforcement should be forced to place their lives in jeopardy because some civilians demand ownership of these highly destructive firearms.

Some argue that while most criminals prefer to use other weapons, assault weapons are more likely to actually be used in crime than are other firearms. According to some estimates before the Assault Weapons Ban, assault weapons accounted for less than 1% of civilian firearms, but up to 11% of guns used in crime[9]. There are, however, some questions about the accuracy of these statistics.

What is most disturbing about assault weapons is that people planning on mass killings, whether in the workplace, a restaurant or school, almost invariably use these weapons rather than a simple handgun. Assault weapons are the weapon of choice and result in far too many casualties, almost inevitably the death of victims due to the high rate of fire. The victims in the Newtown massacre, for instance, had up to nine bullet wounds each, because of an assault weapon.

Obesity Kills More People than Assault Rifles.

Cardiovascular disease, infectious diseases, malignant neoplasm (cancer) and a host of diseases kill a great number of Americans each day. None of which has anything to do with gun deaths. Disease is an unpleasant fact, as is death. The difference is that the majority of people dying of these diseases are elderly, and their bodies do break down over time as their tissues accrue more errors in cell division and as their body's ability to fight disease deteriorates.

Obesity is preventable, but a hamburger-wielding assailant does not kill two-dozen people in minutes. The same people opposing gun restrictions invariably oppose campaigns against fast foods and an unhealthy lifestyle, as witness the Michael Bloomberg ban on soft drinks over 24oz. Government agencies have warned for generations against the health risks of smoking, poor diet and lack of exercise. Attempts to ban smoking or improve the diet of Americans have met universally with derision. This is part of the overarching indifference to life pervading conservative ideology.

Obesity does not kill people, whereas heart disease, stroke or diabetes might, and these are correlated with obesity, but as gun advocates often claim, correlation does not imply causation. Eating a single hamburger is unlikely to lead to your demise; over time, plaque buildup in your arteries might lead to a stroke. With a firearm, it only takes a single bullet to end your life.

Additionally, with obesity, an individual can take action to reduce his or her risk of becoming obese, albeit particularly difficult in a nation with almost universally unhealthy food. That individual has no control over a gun owner entering a restaurant with a semi-automatic weapon and taking a great many lives.

As federal and state budgets are cut, so research into disease prevention is reduced, increasing the chances of premature death from disease, including obesity. Funding into obesity research has been cut from budgets along with other government cuts. The same research into the causes of firearm deaths has been illegal for years.

Among youths aged 15 to 24, gun homicides and suicides exceed deaths by all other causes except accidents, including disease or obesity. Only car accidents currently cause more death among children and young adults. For non-Hispanic black youths, homicide is the single leading cause of death[10].

As a society, we try to mitigate all deaths, regardless of cause. We have agencies like the CDC, FDA, EPA and others all tasked with reducing unnecessary death and injury. Despite its importance, conservatives continually cut funding for research into disease and accident. No single cause of death is more or less important than any other. However, some deaths are so violent, preventable, and unnecessary, that we feel it is our duty to stop them by whatever means we can. This is why we crack down on terrorism and drug gangs.

Obesity is unlikely to lead to the violent overthrow of our democratic system of governance. It is quite likely, given the ubiquity of firearms, that an attempt at the violent overthrow of government will be made using semi-automatic weapons.

The implication here is that because we have a high number of deaths that are linked to obesity because of the stress that overweight puts on society, we should do nothing about assault weapons or firearms. It is as though death by firearm is of no consequence and we can ignore it because we have such other pressing issues as obesity and heart disease.

The Assault Weapon Ban Did Not Work

The years after the federal Assault Weapons Ban saw the number of firearm deaths drop from 38,505 in 1994 to 28,663 in 2000, while the rate dropped from 14.8 to 10.4 per 100,000. Whether the ban was the proximate cause is difficult to tell, but it certainly did no harm and quite possibly benefited society.

A 2012 study found that there was a statistically significant rise in homicides in Mexico subsequent to the 2004 expiration of the Federal Assault Weapons Ban in the U.S. States like Texas, Arizona and New Mexico, which relaxed sales of assault weapons, saw a rise in homicides in Mexican municipalities closest to their borders. California, which retained the ban, saw little change in homicides in those Mexican areas closest to their border[11]. A survey determined that 3% of trafficked guns in Mexico came from California, while 29% came from Arizona and 50% from Texas. Following the expiration of the AWB, Mexico saw their homicide rate rise 45%, with more than 60,000 recovered firearms traced to the U.S. At least 16.4% of the increase can be traced to the expiration[12].

At least 239 additional deaths have accrued each year in Mexico since the 2004 assault weapons ban expired. That is over 2000 additional deaths due to the reluctance of Texas, Arizona and New Mexico to institute an assault weapons ban. Those states plan are unlikely to tell the families of those lost because of their callous disregard for Mexican lives. They are also unlikely to pay reparations to Mexico for their losses.

The assault weapons ban in the U.S. successfully kept assault weapons from falling into the hands of Mexican drug cartels, and saving countless lives. Clearly, the lives lost are unimportant to many American gun owners who place a greater weight on their ostensible right to bear arms than on the right of Mexican citizens to life.

In the U.S., the ban had similar effects, with the crimes involving assault weapons declining by 17% to 72% in studied cities, which included Baltimore, Miami, Milwaukee and others[13]. It is true that assault pistols, which are easier to use, largely replaced assault rifles in crimes, while the common feature is the use of large capacity magazines (LCM), which hold more than 10 rounds and up to 30 rounds. The banning of assault pistols and LCM's would go a long way towards mitigating the death rate in American cities.

Between 1994 and 1995, the criminal use of assault weapons as measured by the ATF, fell 20% compared to 11% for all weapons. However, because of the limited use of these weapons in most murders, the overall impact on homicide was limited, in the U.S.[14]. Despite that, the ban contributed to a 6.7% decrease in murders between 1994 and 1995.

An analysis of attacks in one city determined that 3% of gunfire incidents produced more than 10 fired shots and those attacks produced 5% of gunshot victims. These weapons result in a greater number of shots fired, more people hit and more gunshot wounds than attacks with other firearms[15].

There were aspects of the ban that did not work. Each weapon needed to possess at least two specific military features, whereas the ATF prefers a single military feature for a weapon to be defined as an assault weapon. The transfer and possession of assault weapons manufactured before the ban remained legal, which diluted the bans intent. Many manufacturers redesigned their weapons to circumvent the provisions of the ban by, for instance, removing a military feature without compromising the weapon, or replacing components with items not named under law. The law banned specific firearm copies, but failed to define copies. Lastly, the ban was set to expire in 2004, negating many of the positive contributions of the ban to lower gun violence[16].

California's assault weapon ban was far more effective; it banned 75 types, models and series of weapons; mandated that lawfully owned assault weapons be registered and prohibited transfers within the state. Manufacturers were found to be altering their weapons just enough to evade the ban. California responded to this in 1999, when it modified its requirement to a single military feature in defining assault weapons. Using this standard, almost all semi-automatic weapons designed for rapid, accurate spray firing were banned from the civilian market[17]. In addition, in 2002, the act was modified, requiring the California Department of Justice to conduct an annual security and safe storage inspection of every person, firm or corporation holding a permit to possess or own an assault weapon.

The reduction in the use of assault weapons, especially pistols was largely offset by the use of other weapons using large capacity magazines. The exemption applied to weapons purchased before the ban also diluted the expected reductions in gun crimes using these weapons. A full ban on all assault weapons and large capacity magazines would likely be more effective and save more lives.

Stockpiles of assault weapons that are not included in the ban, or those manufactured before the ban, were still available for purchase through straw sales, theft, or off-the-book sales falsely reported as thefts[18]. These sales can produce an unintended impact on crime that negate the effect of the ban

The expectation that results would be seen immediately on implementation of the ban was also premature. Experiences in other countries that have introduced gun bans found that the bans took a number of years to have an impact, typically three or more years following the ban.

Assault Weapons Guarantee Freedom

I would challenge anyone to find a nation in recent history that guaranteed its freedom from tyrannical government with semi-automatic assault weapons. In every case, almost all found within Africa or Central America, automatic weapons have been used to oppress, control, slaughter, commit genocide, and intimidate the people. In those cases in which armed insurgents, resistance or rebel groups have taken up arms against the government, civilians have overwhelmingly been the victims of both government and rebel forces. This has happened from Angola and Mozambique to Algeria and Somalia.

In those parts of Africa and Central America in which the old Soviet Union armed liberation groups with AK-47s, those weapons were used to impose tyrannical governments on people. Despite widespread gun ownership in those countries, the people remain oppressed. In Central America, the Contras, armed by the United States against the duly elected Sandinistas, viciously oppressed the Nicaraguan people with small armaments. Those small arms did nothing to free the people. Small arms given to rebels in countries like Chile were used to overthrow the democratic government under

Salvador Allende and replace it with a dictatorship under Augusto Pinochet.

Assault weapons in the United States are far more likely to be used to intimidate and persecute people than to ensure their freedom. The increased risk of insurrection may well lead to the nullification of all freedoms if political gridlock, government shutdowns and economic austerity continue on their current path.

Given overwhelming American military force, personal assault rifles are of little value in combating tyrannical government. The military is as likely to impose a totalitarian state as is an extremist government. In the case of armed insurrection, the very real danger is that the military joins with armed civilians, or self-styled militias, to oppress unarmed civilians. That threat is enough to take guns from the civilian population and control military firearm availability. The experience of many nations with paramilitary forces has never been a good one, with many paramilitary forces oppressing their populations with brutality and a lack of mercy.

People sometimes cite public disorder as a reason for assault weapon ownership, for instance in the Los Angeles riots. While there was looting by opportunists, the presence of assault weapons among rioters and bystanders could well have led to a far more serious situation and a great many more deaths. While shop owners may arm themselves, rioters could as easily and legally arm themselves, leading to a deteriorating situation and possible military intervention. As it was, the LA riots disappeared after a few days of their own accord.

Assault weapons are increasingly emerging among drug traffickers, criminal gangs, mass murderers and dangerous criminals. The dangers to civilian society are no less urgent than they are in nations with rebel groups, paramilitaries and other extra-governmental organizations.

Semi Automatic Weapons Can Be Used on a Range

Many gun enthusiasts say that they do not need their assault weapons for self-defense, since there are better options available, but they like to take their weapon to the range to shoot them. As one enthusiast said, "some people play golf, others bowl, I shoot. Every month I take my guns out to the range and shoot... it's fun, exciting and a great way to vent"[19]. I concur. Semi-automatic weapons may be exciting to some people for target shooting.

There is a simple solution to the availability of assault weapons; all military-style assault weapons should be kept on gun ranges, locked up safely away from theft, burglary, irate spouses or anyone bent on harming others. People could go and use their own weapons, kept for them at a range, and fire them to their hearts content. No one is harmed, they get to keep their weapons, and there are no stolen or mislaid weapons on the street. Everyone gains and no one loses.

People could even modify their weapons as they please, as long as those weapons remain on the range. That way, the gun lobby could be satisfied, the gun owners can fire their weapons whenever they want, no animals get slaughtered by irresponsible hunters with assault rifles, no accidental shootings occur at home while cleaning the weapons, and no Adam Lanza's shooting up children in elementary schools.

If a gun enthusiast wants to fire a particular weapon while away from home, there is little to stop him paying his dues at a gun range and hiring their weapons. This is true for skeet shooting, range shooting or anything else.

Assault Weapons Are More Accurate Than Handguns

In a home situation, the person that is unable to use a handgun effectively should think of something other than a weapon to protect his home. If properly taught, a gun owner ought to be able to use a handgun effectively in the home. Everything is short range. There is no rational reason to need an assault weapon. Believing that the only thing that will protect your home effectively is an assault weapon is just ludicrous. Longer weapons are more difficult to deploy in tight urban environments. If you cannot neutralize an intruder with six rounds from a revolver, perhaps you should not have access to weapons.

The idea that a rifle is easier to learn to fire is just as ridiculous. Being able to fire multiple rounds at a target in a tight environment really does not make anyone any safer.

Civilian Assault Weapons Are Not Automatic

Gun rights advocates mislead the public and politicians when it comes to automatic or semi-automatic weapons. The AR-15 has a civilian version that is semi-automatic, which means it requires a pull of the trigger to fire a round. With each round ejected, a new round is pumped into the chamber. Clearly, it cannot fire as many rounds per second as a military assault rifle. However, there are legally available options that do allow for simulated automatic operation. The AR-15 has an accessory known as the Slide Fire Stock, which provides the civilian AR-15 with close to automatic fire[20]. This accessory is freely available and approved by the ATF[21].

Regardless of gun lobby claims, the Bushmaster is marketed as a military weapon, as is demonstrated by gun industry advertising, which says in part[22],

> "Our new Bushmaster ACR redefines the term "modular" with the extraordinary
> ability to change calibers, barrel lengths and stock configurations in minutes –

without the use of tools. Truly the most versatile and adaptive rifle ever conceived, it was born of a collaborative effort between Bushmaster®, Magpul®, and Remington® to create the ultimate military combat weapons system."

Even in standard form, the Bushmaster XM15 manual lists the maximum effective rate of fire at 45 rounds per minute[23], more than enough to enable Adam Lanza to slaughter 26 innocent people. These weapons may not be automatic, but they are rapid-fire weapons. Those children did not ask whether they were dismembered by a military assault rifle, or a civilian assault rifle, the fact is that a civilian armed with a legally obtained firearm was able to massacre these children and their teachers in around five minutes. It matters not one whit what you call these weapons, they should not be in civilian hands.

In a nation like Switzerland, those who serve in the defense forces, and every able-bodied male must do so, are issued with either an assault rifle or a pistol. The assault rifle is modified from automatic to semi automatic. When they leave the service, they may retain their service weapon, but it is modified from semi-automatic to single shot. The same could be done here, with automatic and semi-automatic weapons banned anywhere but a gun range, and all home defense weapons modified for single shot.

There is little qualitative difference between the killing power of a civilian and military assault weapon other than the rate of fire. Many of the functional design features that make assault weapons deadly are present in civilian weapons. Weapons fired on semi-automatic are invariably more accurate than those fired in automatic, making civilian assault weapons as deadly as military weapons. Civilian assault weapons do not display 'cosmetic' features to merely resemble military weapons, many of the functional design features on military weapons are present on their civilian counterparts. The spray-fire capability of military weapons is mimicked in civilian versions allowing for laying down a high-volume of fire over a wide area. There is no justification for this functionality in a civilian setting[24].

Features such as high capacity magazines, rear pistol or thumbhole grip, forward grip or barrel shroud are design features that make assault weapons so deadly to civilian populations. The features banned in the 1994 Assault Weapons Ban were not relevant to the assault weapons functionality; bayonet mounts, grenade launchers, silencers and flash suppressors[25].

An FBI study determined that with experience, a gunman could fire an automatic pistol six times in less than a second. Even an inexperienced novice can fire a semi-automatic handgun three times in 1.5 seconds, or more than a hundred times a minute[26]. Some novices were able to get off three rounds per second.

Assault Weapons Are Great For Home Defense

Bolt-action rifles and shotguns can be used for home defense, too. What has really happened is that gun manufacturers make a lot of money out of the average AR-15, as opposed to the average handgun. The AR-15 and AK-47 are effective at ranges anywhere up to 600 yards or more; additionally, the projectiles are able to penetrate the walls of homes, including the exterior wall in a wood framed home. In a home invasion, using these weapons, it is easy to kill or injure neighbors or other innocent bystanders by shooting wildly at invaders. It is far less likely using a handgun, which has a far shorter range that there would be collateral damage. It is not just the projectile that may cause damage to neighbors, but injuries caused by flying debris that can act as shrapnel[27].

Conclusion

The evidence from every developed nation around the world is abundantly clear. Strict regulation on firearms is highly successful at preventing firearms from falling into the wrong hands. The United States suffers from the collective delusional belief that firearms make for a safer society.

Every massacre is accompanied by a debate resembling a whirlpool; it revolves around a single point, but does not solve much. Just as with debates about evolution, abortion, or the viability of social programs, only vigorous, honest research will verify the truth of either side.

Most countries understand immediately what needs to be done to prevent gun violence, and take action quickly. Only when Americans are able to acknowledge the central truth of gun violence, that more guns and lenient laws increase gun deaths and injuries, will we be able to deal with the problem. Until then, the incessant drip of death and injury will continue.

There are few good reasons to keep firearms, despite the warped interpretation of the Second Amendment. Why so many still cling to these arguments is a question that will plague future historians and cultural scientists?

We must question the morality of our continued obsession with firearms. It cannot be moral to ignore the solution to unwanted death. Are we a moral people, or are we not? That is the central question we need to answer.

Notes

1 Annan, Kofi. 2000. 'Freedom from Fear: Small Arm s.' Report of the Secretary-General to the Millenium Assembly of the United Nations. United Nations General Assem bly, 27 March. (Q 181)

2 UNGA. 1997. 'Report of the Panel of Governmental Experts on Small Arms.' General and Complete Disarmament Small Arms; Note by the Secretary General: A/52/298 (III). p. 11. New York: United Nations General Assembly 27 August. Geneva Declaration. 2008. 'Dimensions of Armed Violence.' Global Burden of Armed Violence, p. 2. Geneva: Geneva Declaration on Armed Violence and Development Secretariat. 12 September.

1 <http://www.gunpolicy.org/firearms/region>. "Global impact of gun violence." UNGA.1997.'Report of the Panel of Governmental Experts on Small Arms.' *General and Complete Disarmament: Small Arms.*New York:United Nations General Assembly,27 August. (Q174)

22 <http://www.theguardian.com/commentisfree/2013/sep/21/american-gun-out-control-porter> . Henry Porter. September 21st, 2013. :American gun use is out of control. Shouldn't the world intervene?"

1 <http://www.americanprogress.org/issues/civil-liberties/report/2013/04/02/58382/america-under-the-gun/>. "America under the gun: A 50 state analysis of gun violence and its link to weak state gun laws." Arkadi Gerney, Chelsea Parsons, Charles Posner. April 2nd, 2013.

2 <http://archinte.jamanetwork.com/article.aspx?articleid=1661390>. "Firearm legislation and firearm related fatalities in the United States." Eric W. Fleegler, MD, MPH; Lois K. Lee, MD, MPH; Michael C. Monuteaux, ScD; David Hemenway, PhD; Rebekah Mannix, MD, MPH. JAMA Intern Med. 2013;173(9):732-740. doi:10.1001/jamainternmed.2013.1286. Published online March 16th, 2013.

3 <http://www.mayorsagainstillegalguns.org/downloads/pdf/trace_the_guns_report.pdf>. "The link between gun laws and insterstate gun trafficking." Mayors Against Illegal Guns. September 2010. From The Law Center to Prevent Gun Violence, November 2012.

4 <www.nytimes.com/2013/04/03/us/report-links-high-rates-of-gun-violence-to-weak-laws.html>. Erica Goode. New York Times. April 2nd, 2013. "Report links high rates og gun violence to weak state regulations."

5 Rates of violent crime: New York State (392), California (440), Louisiana (549). National average (403). Statistics per 100,000

6 <http://www.ucrdatatool.gov/Search/Crime/State/StateCrime.cfm>. Uniform Crime Reporting Statistics, U.S. Department of Justice. Last Accessed June 19th, 2013.

7 Rates of violent crime: Arkansas (480), Missouri (447), New Mexico (567), South Carolina (572)

8 New York City Crime Rate (593) per 100,000.

9 Violent Crime Rate Houston, Texas, (1,071 per 100,000)

10 <http://www.visionofhumanity.org/pdf/uspi/2012-US-Peace-Index-Media-Release.pdf>. Institute for Economics and peace. "2012 U.S. peace index highlights Americans most and least peaceful cities and states." Michael Shank, Craig Brownstein. April 24th, 2012.

11 Journal of the American Medical Association, 1996.

12 <http://www.bradynetwork.org/site/DocServer/PATH_FAQ.pdf?docID=361> Accessed October28th, 2013.

13 <http://www.americanprogress.org/issues/civil-liberties/report/2013/04/02/58382/america-under-the-gun/>. "America under the gun: A 50 state analysis of gun violence and its link to weak state gun laws." Arkadi Gerney, Chelsea Parsons, Charles Posner. April 2nd, 2013.

14 <http://www.mayorsagainstillegalguns.org/downloads/pdf/trace_the_guns_report.pdf>.

"The link between gun laws and insterstate gun trafficking." Mayors Against Illegal Guns. September 2010.

[15] <http://www.mayorsagainstillegalguns.org/downloads/pdf/inside-straw-purchases.pdf> Accessed October 14th, 2013. "Inside straw purchasing: How criminals get guns illegally". Mayors Against Illegal Guns.

[16] ibid.

[17] <http://www.mayorsagainstillegalguns.org/downloads/pdf/trace_the_guns_report.pdf>. "The link between gun laws and insterstate gun trafficking." Mayors Against Illegal Guns. September 2010.

[18] <http://usliberals.about.com/od/Election2012Factors/a/Gun-Owners-As-Percentage-Of-Each-States-Population.htm>, Last Accessed 27th, 2013. "Gun owners as percentage of Each State's Population".

[19] High Gun Ownership Rates Wyoming (59.7%), Alaska (57.8%), Montana (57.7%), South Dakota (56.6%), West Virginia (55.4%) and Mississippi (55.3%), Gun Death Rates: Alaska (20), Wyoming (18.8), Montana (14.5). South Dakota (7.9), West Virginia (14.7), Mississippi (17.3).

[20] Low Gun Ownership Rates: Hawaii (6.7%), New Jersey (12.3%), Massachusetts (12.6%), Rhode Island (12.8%), Connecticut (16.7%), New York (18%). Gun Death Rates: Hawaii (2.8), New Jersey (4.9), Massachusetts (3.1), Rhode Island (5.1), Connecticut (4.3), New York (5.1).

[21] <http://www.theatlanticcities.com/neighborhoods/2012/07/geography-gun-violence/2655/> Richard Florida, July 20th, 2012, "The Geography of gun Violence".

[22] <http://www.americanprogress.org/issues/civil-liberties/report/2013/04/02/58382/america-under-the-gun/> . "America Under the Gun: A 50-state analysis of gun violence and its link to weak state gun laws." Arkadi Gerney, Chelsea Parsons, Charles Posner. Last accessed July 11th, 2013. April 2nd, 2013.

[23] <http://www.theatlantic.com/national/archive/2011/01/the-geography-of-gun-deaths/69354/> , Richard Florida, January 13th, 2011. "The Geography of Gun Deaths".

[24] Metro Areas with highest death rates: New Orleans (32.8), Birmingham (20.5) and Memphis (19.8)

[25] Metro Areas with lowest death rates: Providence (4.1), San Jose (3.8) and Boston (3.6)

[26] Cities with highest death rates: Detroit (41.4), Las Vegas (36.9) and Miami (33.5)

[27] Cities with lowest death rates: San Diego (7.1), New York City (4.9) and San Jose (4.0)

[28] <http://www.theatlanticcities.com/neighborhoods/2012/12/geography-us-gun-violence/4171/> Richard Florida, December 14th, 2012. "The Geography of Gun Violence".

[29] <http://www.americanprogress.org/issues/civil-liberties/report/2013/04/02/58382/america-under-the-gun/>. "America under the gun: A 50 state analysis of gun violence and its link to weak state gun laws." Arkadi Gerney, Chelsea Parsons, Charles Posner. April 2nd, 2013.

[30] <http://www.americanprogress.org/issues/civil-liberties/report/2013/04/02/58382/america-under-the-gun/>. "America under the gun: A 50 state analysis of gun violence and its link to weak state gun laws." Arkadi Gerney, Chelsea Parsons, Charles Posner. April 2nd, 2013..

[31] Most Dangerous States for Women: Nevada (2.62), South Carolina(1.94), Tennessee (1.91), Louisiana (1.6), Virginia (1.77) and Texas (1.75)

[32] Least Dangerous SAtates for Women: South Dakota (0.25), Illinois (0.32), Minnesota (0.52), and New Hampshire (0.6)

[33] <http://www.vpc.org/studies/wmmw2012.pdf> . "When men murder women: An analysis of 2010 homicide data.". Violence Policy Center. September 2012.

[34] <http://www.mayorsagainstillegalguns.org/html/media-center/pr016-13.shtml>. "Women and guns: new ad and research shows how weak gun laws turn domestic abuse into murder." Mayors Against Illegal Guns. April 3rd, 2013, No. 16.

[35] < http://indianapublicmedia.org/news/indiana-gun-deaths-vehicle-deaths-2009-30664/ > . May 23rd, 2012. "Indiana had more gun deaths than vehicle deaths in 2012". Lauren Glapa.

[1] < http://www.ncbi.nlm.nih.gov/pubmed/1669841 > . Loftin C, McDowall D, Wiersema B, et al. Effects of restrictive licensing of handguns on homicide and suicide in the District of Columbia. N Engl J Med 1991;325:1615–20.

[2] <http://www.bloomberg.com/news/print/2012-12-16/ban-on-30-round-gun-magazines-in-connecticut-died-after-pressure.html>. Michael C. Bender. December 17th, 2012. "Connecticut's 30-bullet magazine ban failed after pressure."

[3] <http://smartgunlaws.org/connecticut-state-law-summary/> , January 2nd, 2012. "Connecticut State Law Summary".

[4] <http://www.pewstates.org/projects/stateline/headlines/as-sandy-hook-students-return-to-school-connecticut-governor-to-launch-gun-violence-task-force-85899440206>, Jim Malewitz, January 4th, 2013, "As Sandy Hook Students return to School, Connecticut governor to Launch Gun Violence Task Force".

[5] <http://www.bloomberg.com/news/print/2012-12-16/ban-on-30-round-gun-magazines-in-connecticut-died-after-pressure.html>. Michael C. bender. December 17th, 2012. "Connecticut's 30-bullet magazine ban failed after pressure."

[6] <http://www.bloomberg.com/news/print/2012-12-16/ban-on-30-round-gun-magazines-in-connecticut-died-after-pressure.html>. Michael C. bender. December 17th, 2012. "Connecticut's 30-bullet magazine ban failed after pressure.".

[7] < http://articles.latimes.com/2013/feb/16/business/la-fi-hiltzik-20130214 >. Michael Hiltzik. February 16th, 2013. "Taking aim at the gun industry."

[8] < http://articles.latimes.com/2013/feb/16/business/la-fi-hiltzik-20130214 > . Michael Hiltzik. February 16th, 2013. "Taking aim at the gun industry.".

[9] <http://en.wikipedia.org/wiki/Cleveland_Elementary_School_shooting_(Stockton)>. Last accessed July 16th, 2013.

[10] <http://en.wikipedia.org/wiki/Roberti-Roos_Assault_Weapons_Control_Act_of_1989> . Last Accessed July 16th, 2013.

[11] <http://articles.latimes.com/1989-05-19/news/mn-112_1_assault-weapons-ban-military-style-assault-types-of-semiautomatic-rifles/2> . Carl Ingram. May 19th, 1989. "Assault gun ban wins final vote: Deukmejian's promised approval would make it first such U.S. law."

[12] < http://articles.latimes.com/2013/feb/16/business/la-fi-hiltzik-20130214 >. Michael Hiltzik. February 16th, 2013. "Taking aim at the gun industry."

[13] <http://www.boston.com/news/local/massachusetts/2013/01/03/mass-lawmakers-weigh-tough-gun-control-measures/K9csk0xCujuLsreIegsXuL/story.html> , Steve LeBlanc, Boston.com news, January 3rd, 2013, "Mass. Lawmakers weigh tough gun control measures."

[14] <http://www.boston.com/news/local/massachusetts/2013/01/03/mass-lawmakers-weigh-tough-gun-control-measures/K9csk0xCujuLsreIegsXuL/story.html> , Steve LeBlanc, Boston.com news, January 3rd, 2013, "Mass. Lawmakers weigh tough gun control measures.".

[15] <http://www.boston.com/news/local/massachusetts/2013/01/03/mass-lawmakers-weigh-tough-gun-control-measures/K9csk0xCujuLsreIegsXuL/story.html> , Steve LeBlanc, Boston.com news, January 3rd, 2013, "Mass. Lawmakers weigh tough gun control measures.".

16 <http://www.denverpost.com/breakingnews/ci_22216076/gov-hickenlooper-pitches-swift-holds-gun-sales-mentally> . Michael Booth. December 19th, 2012. "Gov. Hickenlooper pitches swift holds of gun sales to mentally ill."

17 <http://www.huffingtonpost.com/2013/03/20/colorado-gun-control-laws_n_2917490.html>. March 20th, 2013. Christina Wilkie. "Colorado governor signs landmark gun control laws in blow to NRA."

18 < http://www.denverpost.com/breakingnews/ci_22817663/weld-sheriffs-refusal-enforce-gun-rules-within-letter > . Ryan Parker. March 18th, 2013. Denver Post. "Weld Sheriffs refusal to enforce gun rules within letter of the law."

19 <http://www.nraila.org/DefendCO>, Last accessed 22nd March, 2013.

20 <http://www.americanprogress.org/issues/civil-liberties/report/2013/04/02/58382/america-under-the-gun/> Arkadi Gerney, Chelsea Parsons, Charles Posner. April 2nd, 2013. "America under the gun: A 50-state analysis of gun violence and its link to weak state gun laws."

21 < http://www.motherjones.com/mojo/2013/03/felons-gun-rights-unconstitutional-louisiana > . Deanna Pan. March 25th, 2013. "Louisiana judge rules thatviolent felons have gun rights too."

22 < http://thinkprogress.org/justice/2013/03/22/1763301/court-cites-newly-enacted-louisiana-amendment-to-strike-down-ban-on-felon-gun-possession/ > . Nicole Flatow. March 22nd, 2013. "Court cites newly enacted Louisiana Amendment to strike down ben on felon gun possession.".

23 <http://www.americanprogress.org/issues/civil-liberties/report/2013/04/02/58382/america-under-the-gun/> Arkadi Gerney, Chelsea Parsons, Charles Posner. April 2nd, 2013. "America under the gun: A 50-state analysis of gun violence and its link to weak state gun laws."

1 "The Gun Control Debate" Edited by Lee Nisbet. Prometheus Books, 2001.

2 <http://www.gunpolicy.org/firearms/region/united-states>, "United States - Gun Facts, Figures and the Law > Death and Injury > Total Gun Deaths". Last accessed April 3rd, 2013.

3 <https://www.ncjrs.gov/App/publications/abstract.aspx?ID=187198>. John van Kesteren, Pat Mayhew, Paul Nieuwbeerta. February 2001. "Criminal victimization in seventeen industrialized countries: Key findings from the 2000 International Crime Victims Survey."

4 Special Rapporteur on violence against women, its causes and consequences (U.N. Doc. E/CN.4/1996/53, §32-33). See also, Special Rapporteur on human rights and small arms (U.N. Doc. E/CN.4/Sub.2/2002/39; 5/ 2002). See Also, Eighth Annual Report of Domestic Violence Death Review Committee 2010.

5 <http://www.ncbi.nlm.nih.gov/pubmed/20571454>. Richardson, EG, Hemenway D. "Homicide, suicide and unintentional firearm fatality: Comparing the United States with other high income countries, 2003." January 2011. Last accessed July 18th, 2013.

6 Specific Human Rights Issues: Prevention of human rights violations committed with small arms and light weapons." Barbara Frey, Special Rapporteur in accordance with Sub-Commission resolution 2002/25.

7 Bandeira AR. "Brazil – Gun control and homicide reduction," pages 213-222 in *Reducing Gun Violence in America: Informing Policy with Evidence and Analysis,* Daniel W. Webster and Jon S. Vernick, Eds., Baltimore, MD: Johns Hopkins University Press, 2013.

8 Bandeira AR. "Brazil – Gun control and homicide reduction," pages 213-222 in *Reducing Gun Violence in America: Informing Policy with Evidence and*

Analysis, Daniel W. Webster and Jon S. Vernick, Eds., Baltimore, MD: Johns Hopkins University Press, 2013.

[9] Small Arms Survey 2006, Chapter 8.

[10] <http://www.parl.gc.ca/Content/SEN/Committee/411/lcjc/PDF/Briefs/C19/DEVILL-EN.pdf>. Last accessed July 18th, 2013. "Costs of gun violence and the impact on victims."

[11] <http://en.wikipedia.org/wiki/Montreal_massacre#Gun_control> . Last Accessed July 18th, 2013.

[12] <http://www.visionofhumanity.org/pdf/gpi/2013_Global_Peace_Index_Report.pdf>. Last Accessed July 18th, 2013. "Global Peace Index 2013."

[13] <http://en.wikipedia.org/wiki/List_of_countries_by_guns_and_homicide> , "List of countries by guns and homicide." Last Accessed, 2nd April, 2013.

[14] <http://www.gunpolicy.org/firearms/region/south-africa> , "Death and Injury: Gun Homicides".

[15] <http://www.africacheck.org/reports/did-gun-control-cause-fall-in-gun-crime-the-data-backs-the-claim/>, Ntombi Dyosop. 15th December, 2012. "Did gun control cause fall in gun crime? The data backs the claim."

[16] <http://www.saps.gov.za/statistics/reports/crimestats/2013/downloads/crime_statistics_presentation.pdf>, Last accessed 2nd April, 2012. Crime Statistics overview RSA 2012/13

[17] <http://www.africacheck.org/reports/did-gun-control-cause-fall-in-gun-crime-the-data-backs-the-claim/>, Ntombi Dyosop. 15th December, 2012. "Did gun control cause fall in gun crime? The data backs the claim."

[18] <http://www.mrc.ac.za/crime/nimss.htm> , Last Accessed 2nd April, 2013. "The National Injury Mortality Surveillance System."

[19] http://www.ncbi.nlm.nih.gov/pubmed/21034205 . Lubin G, Werbeloff N, Shmushkevitch M, Weiser M, Knobler HY. 2010 Oct. 40(5):421-4. doi: 10.1521/suli.2010.40.5.421. Division of Mental health, Medical Corps, IDF, Ramat Gan, Israel. "Decrease in suicide rates after a change of policy reducing access to firearms in adolescents: a naturalistic epidemiological study."

[20] <http://ajp.psychiatryonline.org/article.aspx?articleID=1722046>. Reisch, Thomas, M.D. et al. "Change in suicide rates in Sweitzerland before and after firearm restriction resulting from the 2003 'Army XXI' reform."

[21] <http://www.gunpolicy.org/firearms/region/israel>, Last Accessed April 5th, 2013. "Israel – Gun Facts, Figures and the Law > Death and Injury > Gun Homicides"

[22] <http://www.gunpolicy.org/firearms/region/israel>, Last Accessed April 5th, 2013. "Israel – Gun Facts, Figures and the Law > Gun Regulation > Gun Owner Licensing"

[23] < http://www.jpost.com/Israel-News/Politics-And-Diplomacy/For-or-against-easing-gun-controls-neither-side-wants-an-Israeli-Second-Amendment-445402 > "For or Against Easing Gun Controls, Neither Side Wants an Israeli Second Amendmend", Jerusalem Post, 18th February 2016, by Lahav Harkov.

[24] <http://www.gunpolicy.org/firearms/region/japan>, Last Accessed April 2nd, 2013. "Japan – gun facts, figures and the law > Death and Injury > Gun Homicides"

[25] <http://www.theatlantic.com/international/archive/2012/07/a-land-without-guns-how-japan-has-virtually-eliminated-shooting-deaths/260189/> , Max Fisher. July 23rd, 2012. "A land without guns: How Japan has virtually eliminated shooting deaths".

[26] <http://en.wikipedia.org/wiki/Samurai#Decline>, Last Accessed April 2nd, 2013. "Samurai:Decline"

[27] <http://www.guncite.com/journals/dkjgc.html> , David Kopel. Copyright 1993. "Japanese Gun Control."

28
<http://en.wikipedia.org/wiki/Gun_politics_in_Australia#The_Port_Arthur_massacre_an
d_its_consequences>, "Gun Politics in Australia: The Port Arthur Massacre and its
Consequences."
[29] <http://en.wikipedia.org/wiki/Gun_politics#Worldwide_politics_and_legislation> ,
Last Accessed 23rd March, 2013. Gun Politics: Worldwide politics and legislation".
[30] <http://en.wikipedia.org/wiki/Gun_politics_in_Australia> . Last accessed September
24th, 2013.
[31] <http://www.gunpolicy.org/firearms/region/cp/australia> . Last accessed September
24th, 2013. "The big melt: How one democracy changed after scrapping a third of its
firearms." Philip Alpers.
[32] <http://www.gunpolicy.org/firearms/region/australia>, Last accessed, 2nd April, 2013.
"Death and Injury: Total Gun Deaths".
33

<http://en.wikipedia.org/wiki/Gun_politics_in_Australia#Changes_in_social_problems_r
elated_to_firearms_over_time> , Last Accessed 3rd April, 2013. "Gun Politics in
Australia: Changes in Social problems related to firearms over time". Ref. Australian
Bureau of Statistics (2 December 2003)."3309.0.55.001 – Suicides: Recent Trends,
Australia, 1992 to 2002".
[34] <http://www.gunpolicy.org/firearms/region/australia> , "Australia - Gun Facts, Figures
and the Law > Death and Injury > Total Gun Deaths.". Last Accessed 3rd April 2013.
[35] <http://guncontrol.org.au/> , Last Access 3rd April, 2013. "Our strict gun laws have
saved thousands of lives."
36

<http://en.wikipedia.org/wiki/Gun_politics_in_Australia#Statements_by_organisations> ,
Last Access April 3rd, 2013. "Gun politics in Australia: Statements by organizations."
[37] <http://www.wnd.com/2000/03/1951/> , Jon Dougherty. April 24th, 2000. "Australia
shoots back at NRA."
38

<http://www.hsph.harvard.edu/hicrc/files/2013/01/bulletins_australia_spring_2011.pdf>.
Bulletins Spring 2011 (Issue 4). "The Australian Gun Buyback.". Harvard Injury Control
Research Center.
[39] <http://guncontrol.org.au/>. Last Accessed 3rd April 2013. "Brothers in arms, yes, but
the US needs to get rid of its guns."
[40] <http://www.motherjones.com/politics/2012/07/mass-shootings-map>. Mark Follman,
Gavin Aronsen, Deanna Pan. February 27th, 2013. "A Guide to Mass Shootings in
America".
[41] <http://injuryprevention.bmj.com/content/10/5/280.full> . J Ozanne-Smith, K Ashby, S
Newstead, V Z Stathakis, A Clapperton. "Firearm related deaths: the impact of regulatory
reform." Last accessed July 18th, 2013.
[42] < http://www.fbi.gov/about-us/cjis/ucr/crime-in-the-u.s/2010/crime-in-the-u.s.-
2010/violent-crime/violent-crime>. Violent Crime: definition. Last accessed 4th
February, 2014.
[43] <

https://www.gov.uk/government/uploads/system/uploads/attachment_data/file/116226/us
er-guide-crime-statistics.pdf>
[44] <http://www.guardian.co.uk/commentisfree/2013/apr/28/crime-is-down-what-a-
mystery>. Andrew Rawnsley. April 27th, 2013. "A crime mystery: Its going down, but
no one really knows why.". Additional references can be found in the UK Peace Index for
2013, published by the Institute for Economics and Peace.

---

[45] <http://www.visionofhumanity.org/pdf/ukpi/UK_Peace_Index_report_2013.pdf> . "UK Peace Index 2013". Institute for Economics and Peace. Last accessed July 18th, 2013.

[46] <http://www.visionofhumanity.org/pdf/ukpi/UK_Peace_Index_report_2013.pdf> . "UK Peace Index 2013". Institute for Economics and Peace. Last accessed July 18th, 2013.

[47] <http://en.wikipedia.org/wiki/Police_use_of_firearms_in_the_United_Kingdom>. Last Accessed July 18th, 2013.

[48]

<http://en.wikipedia.org/wiki/List_of_British_police_officers_killed_in_the_line_of_dut y> . Last Accessed July 18th, 2013.

[49] <http://www.odmp.org/search/year/2012>. "Honoring officers killed in 2012." Last accessed July 18th, 2013.

[50] <http://en.wikipedia.org/wiki/Amadou_Diallo>. Last accessed July 19th, 2013.

[51] <http://mxgm.org/wp-content/uploads/2012/07/07_24_Report_all_rev_protected.pdf> . Last accessed July 19th, 2013. "Report on the extrajudicial killings of 120 black people, January 1 to June 30, 2012"

[52] <http://en.wikipedia.org/wiki/Gun_politics_in_Switzerland>, Last Accessed April 5th, 2013.

[53] <http://www.gunpolicy.org/firearms/region/switzerland>, Last Accessed April 5th, 2013. Death and Injury > Gun Homicides.

[54] ,http://www.gunpolicy.org/firearms/citation/quotes/1640> , Last Accessed April 5th, 2013.

[55] ,http://www.gunpolicy.org/firearms/region/switzerland>, Last Accessed April 5th, 2013. Gun Regulation > Prohibited Firearms and Ammunition. See citation: <http://www.gunpolicy.org/firearms/citation/quotes/1536>

[56] <http://www.gunpolicy.org/firearms/citation/quotes/1538> , Last Accessed April 5th, 2013.

[1] <http://www.gunpolicy.org/firearms/region/cp/australia> . Philip Alpers. "The big melt: How one democracy changd after scrapping a third of its firearms."

[2] <http://www.bloomberg.com/news/2012-12-19/american-gun-deaths-to-exceed-traffic-fatalities-by-2015.html>. Chris Christoff & IlanKolet. December 19th, 2012.

[3] <http://www.wolframalpha.com/input/?i=us+auto+miles+driven+per+year>. Last Accessed April 30th, 2013.

[4] Haddon W. A logical framework for categorizing highway safety phenomena and activity. *J Trauma.* 1972; 12:193.

[5] <http://www.ncbi.nlm.nih.gov/pubmed/16434012>. "Is an armed society a polite society? Guns and road rage." Hemenway D, Vriniotis M, Miller M. July 2006. Harvard Injury Control Research Center, Harvard School of Public Health..

[6] <http://www.huffingtonpost.com/2013/01/11/james-yeager-gun-ceo_n_2460452.html>. January 11th, 2013. "James Yaeger, CEO who threatened to 'start killing people' over gun control, backpedals...sort of."

[7] <http://opinionator.blogs.nytimes.com/2014/02/15/one-nation-under-guard/?ref=opinion>. New York Times. Samuel Bowles and Arjun Jaayadev. February 15h, 2014. "One Nation Under Guard."

[8] Alba and Messner 1995, pp. 397-402; also see Cook 1991; Zimring 1968

[9] <http://www.pbs.org/opb/historydetectives/technique/gun-timeline/>, PBS, "Gun Timeline". Last Accessed April 5th, 2013.

[10] <http://hhshootingsports.com/WireShots/archives/3601>, Wireshots Staff. Feb 26th, 2013. "The AR-15 is more than a gun. It's a gadget."

[11] <http://en.wikipedia.org/wiki/Rwandan_massacre#Genocide> , Last Accessed April 4th, 2013. "Rwandan Massacre > Genocide".

[12] <http://www.pewstates.org/projects/stateline/headlines/another-mass-shooting-revives-debate-on-gun-laws-85899436948>, Jim Malewitz, December 17th, 2012. "Another Mass Shooting Revives Debate on Gun Control".

[13] <http://www.salon.com/2013/01/11/stop_talking_about_hitler/> . Alex Seitz-Wald. January 11th, 2013. "The Hitler gun control lie." Also see Guns, Crime and Freedom by Wayne LaPierre, publ. Regnery Publishing, 1st Ed. Jun 27th,1994.

[14] <http://www.firstworldwar.com/source/versailles159-213.htm>. Last Accessed August 5th, 2013. "Treaty of Versailles: Articles 159-213." Also, http://net.lib.byu.edu/~rdh7/wwi/versa/versa4.html

[15] <http://tobacco.health.usyd.edu.au/assets/pdfs/Other-Research/2006InjuryPrevent.pdf> . S Chapman, P Alpers, , K Agho, M Jones. "Australia's 1996 gun law reforms: faster falls in firearm deaths, firearm suicides and a decade without mass shootings." Last accessed August 8th, 2013.

[16] <http://www.motherjones.com/politics/2012/07/mass-shootings-map>. Mark Follman, Gavin Aronsen, Deanna Pan. February 27th, 2013. "A guide to mass shootings in America."

[17] <http://www.motherjones.com/politics/2012/07/mass-shootings-map>. Mark Follman, Gavin Aronsen, Deanna Pan. February 27th, 2013. "A guide to mass shootings in America.".

[18] http://alecexposed.org/w/images/6/64/7J12-Resolution_on_the_Second_Amendment_to_the_U_Exposed.pdf , Last Accessed 27th March, 2013.

[19] The figures given in this section are from the David Hemenway report, "Survey research and self-defense gun use: An explanation of extreme overestimates." Much of the wording is from that source, although I intersperse my own thoughts within the paragraphs.

20 Professors Gary Kleck and Marc Gertz, "Armed Resistance to Crime: The Prevalence and Nature of Self-Defense with a Gun", 86 J. Crim. & Criminology 150 (1995)

[21] <http://www.saf.org/lawreviews/hemenway1.htm>, Last Accessed April 6th, 2013. "Survey Research and self defense gun use: An explanation of extreme overestimates."

[22] < http://www.fbi.gov/about-us/cjis/ucr/crime-in-the-u.s/2010/crime-in-the-u.s.-2010/offenses-known-to-law-enforcement/expanded/expandhomicidemain> Last accessed February 27th, 2014.

[23] <http://www.saf.org/lawreviews/hemenway1.htm> , Last Accessed April 6th, 2013. "Survey Research and self defense gun use: An explanation of extreme overestimates.".

[24] <http://www.saf.org/lawreviews/hemenway1.htm> , Last Accessed April 6th, 2013. "Survey Research and self defense gun use: An explanation of extreme overestimates.".

[25] <http://www.saf.org/lawreviews/hemenway1.htm> , Last Accessed April 6th, 2013. "Survey Research and self defense gun use: An explanation of extreme overestimates.". <http://www.saf.org/lawreviews/hemenway1.htm> , Last Accessed April 6th, 2013. "Survey Research and self defense gun use: An explanation of extreme overestimates.".

[27] <http://www.saf.org/lawreviews/hemenway1.htm> , Last Accessed April 6th, 2013. "Survey Research and self defense gun use: An explanation of extreme overestimates.". <http://www.saf.org/lawreviews/hemenway1.htm> , Last Accessed April 6th, 2013. "Survey Research and self defense gun use: An explanation of extreme overestimates.".

29 < http://www.prisonpolicy.org/scans/bjs/femvied.pdf >. Ronet Bachman & Linda E. Saltzman, U.S. Dep't. of Justice, Violence Against Women: Estimates from the Redesigned Survey (1995); Bureau of Justice Statistics, Sourcebook of Criminal Justice

Statistics, 320 tbl.3.1 (1994).

30 David Hemenway, Guns, Public Health and Public Safety, in Guns and the Constitution 49, 64 (Dennis A. Henigan et al. eds., 1995).

[31] <http://www.saf.org/lawreviews/hemenway1.htm>, Last Accessed April 6th, 2013. "Survey Research and self defense gun use: An explanation of extreme overestimates."

[32] < http://www.ncbi.nlm.nih.gov/pubmed/7769767 >. See Joseph A. Annest et al., National Estimates of Nonfatal Firearm-Related Injuries: Beyond the Tip of the Iceberg, 273 JAMA 1749 (1995).

[33] <http://www.bjs.gov/content/pub/pdf/fv9311.pdf>. "Firearm violence, 1993-2011." U.S. Department of Justice. May 2013. Michael Planty (PhD), Jennifer L. Truman (PhD).

[34] <http://scienceblogs.com/deltoid/2000/01/01/duncan1/> . Otis Dudley Duncan, U.C Santa Barbara. January 1st, 2000. "Gun use surveys: In numbers we trust."

[35] <http://scienceblogs.com/deltoid/2000/01/01/duncan1/>. Otis Dudley Duncan, U.C Santa Barbara. January 1st, 2000. "Gun use surveys: In numbers we trust.".

[36] http://en.wikipedia.org/wiki/United_States_prison_population , "Incarceration in the United States". Last accessed 2nd April, 2013.

[37] <

http://pricetheory.uchicago.edu/levitt/Papers/LevittUnderstandingWhyCrime2004.pdf >. Levitt, S. Understanding why crime fell in the 1990s: Four factors that explain the decline and six that do not. Journal of Economic Perspectives. 2004; 18(1):163-190.

[38] Blumestein and Wallman. Blumestein A, Rosenfeld R. Assessing the recent ups and downs in US homicide rates. *National Institute of Justice Journal*, October 1998, 9-11. Full article available: *Journal of Law and Criminology*, 1998; 88(4). Also See Blumstein A, Wallman J. The crime drop and beyond. *Annual Review of Law. Soc. Sci.* 2006. 2:215-46.

[39] Nevin R. Understanding international crime trends: the legacy of preschool lead exposure. Enfron Res. 2007; 104(3):315-336.

[40] < http://www.ncbi.nlm.nih.gov/pmc/articles/PMC2866619/ >. Cerda M Messner S, Tracy M, et al. Investigating the effect of social changes on age-specific gun-related homicide rates in New York City during the 1990s. American Journal of Public Health. 2010; 100(6): 1107-1115.

[41] <http://www.plosmedicine.org/article/info:doi/10.1371/journal.pmed.0050101>. John Paul Wright, Kim N Dietrich. "Association of prenatal and childhood blood lead concentrations with criminal arrests in childhood."

[42] <http://factsanddetails.com/japan.php?itemid=816>, "Crime in Japan.". Last Accessed 2nd April, 2013.

[43] < http://www.fbi.gov/stats-services/crimestats >. FBI Uniform Crime Reports,2001.

[44] < http://www.ncbi.nlm.nih.gov/pmc/articles/PMC2866619/ >. Cerda M Messner S, Tracy M, et al. Investigating the effect of social changes on age-specific gun-related homicide rates in New York City during the 1990s. American Journal of Public Health. 2010; 100(6): 1107-1115.

[45] <http://www.nytimes.com/2013/03/10/us/rate-of-gun-ownership-is-down-survey-shows.html?pagewanted=1&_r=1>, Sabrina Tavernise and Robert Gebelhoff, March 9th, 2013. Statistics obtained from the General Social Survey of the independent research organization NORC.

[46] <http://www.nytimes.com/2013/03/10/us/rate-of-gun-ownership-is-down-survey-shows.html?pagewanted=1&_r=1>, Sabrina Tavernise and Robert Gebelhoff, March 9th, 2013. Statistics obtained from the General Social Survey of the independent research organization NORC..

[47] <http://injuryprevention.bmj.com/content/13/1/15.full>, L. Hepburn, M. Miller, D.

Azrael, D Hemenway. October 4th, 2006. Inj Prev 2007;**13**:15-19 doi:10.1136/ip.2006.013607. Volume 13 Issue 1.

[48] <http://www.theatlanticwire.com/politics/2012/12/guns-in-america-statistics/60071/> Elspeth Reeve, December 17th, 2012. "Some uncomfortable Numbers about Guns in America." The Atlantic Wire.

[49] <http://www.theatlantic.com/international/archive/2012/07/a-land-without-guns-how-japan-has-virtually-eliminated-shooting-deaths/260189/> , Max Fisher. July 22nd, 2012. "A land without guns: how Japan has virtually eliminated shooting deaths."

[50] <http://news.bbc.co.uk/2/hi/asia-pacific/7257072.stm>, Chris Hogg, BBC News, Tokyo. February 27th, 2008. "Gun Crimes Rise Alarms Japanese".

[51] <http://en.wikipedia.org/wiki/2011_Norway_attacks#Preparation_for_the_attacks>, Last Accessed April 8th, 2013. "2011 Norway Attacks: Preparation for the attacks".

[52] <http://www.telegraph.co.uk/news/worldnews/europe/norway/8660986/Norway-shooting-Glenn-Beck-compares-dead-teenagers-to-Hitler-youth.html> , Jon Swaine, New York. The Telegraph. July 25th, 2011.

[53] <http://andrewleigh.org/pdf/GunBuyback_Panel.pdf>. Andrew Leigh, Christine Neill. "Do gun buybacks save lives."

[54] http://www.time.com/time/world/article/0,8599,1993727,00.html . Nick Assinder. June 3rd. 2010. "Shootings reignite gun control debate in Britain."

[55] <http://www.gunpolicy.org/firearms/compare/194/rate_of_gun_homicide/10,192,31>. Last accessed August 8th, 2013.

[56] <http://www.bloomberg.com/news/2013-02-07/gun-background-checks-work-let-s-fund-them-.html>. Frank A.S. Campbell. February 7t, 2013. "Gun background checks work: Lets fund them."

[57] <http://www.bloomberg.com/news/2013-02-07/gun-background-checks-work-let-s-fund-them-.html> . Frank A.S. Campbell. February 7t, 2013. "Gun background checks work: Lets fund them."

[58] <http://www.mcclatchydc.com/2013/03/12/185595/poll-americans-want-background.html#.UgVWi5LUnN4>. David Lightman. March 12th, 2013. "Poll: Americans want background checks for guns, ban on assault weapons."

[59] <http://www.buzzfeed.com/stevefriess/how-the-nra-built-a-massive-secret-database-of-gun-owners>. Steve Friess. August 20th, 2013. "How the NRA built a massive secret database of gun owners."

[60] <http://www.buzzfeed.com/stevefriess/how-the-nra-built-a-massive-secret-database-of-gun-owners>. Steve Friess. August 20th, 2013. "How the NRA built a massive secret database of gun owners".

[61] <http://www.cnn.com/2012/07/20/politics/gun-politics/index.html> , Dana Bash. CNN Senior Congressional Correspondent. July 20th, 2012. "For Democrats, Gun Politics are Bad Politics".

[62] <http://www.thedailybeast.com/articles/2013/05/26/adam-lanza-never-would-have-been-able-to-get-his-hands-on-an-illegal-firearm.html>. Matthew Parker. May 26th, 2013. "The NRA is wrong: The myth of illegal guns."

[63] <http://gunvictimsaction.org/fact-sheet/fact-sheet-illegal-gun-trafficking-arms-criminals-and-youth/>. National Gun Victims Action Council. Last accessed August 8th, 2013.

[64] <http://www.pbs.org/wgbh/pages/frontline/shows/guns/procon/guns.html>. Dan Noyes. "How criminals get guns." Last accessed August 8th, 2013.

[65] <http://www.pbs.org/wgbh/pages/frontline/shows/guns/procon/guns.html>. Dan Noyes. "How criminals get guns." Last accessed August 8th, 2013..

[66] <http://www.atf.gov/publications/historical/ycgii/ycgii-report-2000.html>. Last

---

Accessed August 8th, 2013. Bureau of Alcohol, Tobacco and Firearms (ATF). *Crime Gun Trace Reports (2000): The Youth Gun Interdiction Initiative.* Washington, DC: U.S. Department of the Treasury; 2002.

[67] <http://injuryprevention.bmj.com/content/9/2/147.full>. Sorenson SB, Vittes KA. Buying a handgun for someone else: Firearm dealers' willingness to sell. Inj Prev. 2003; 9: 147–150.

[68] <http://www.ncbi.nlm.nih.gov/pmc/articles/PMC2586780/>. Webster DW, Bulzacchelli MT, Zeoli AM, Vernick JS. "Effects of undercover police stings of gun dealers on the supply of new guns to criminals." Inj Prev. 2006; 12: 225–230.

[69] <http://www.ncbi.nlm.nih.gov/pmc/articles/PMC2704273/>. Daniel W Webster, Jon S. Vernick, Maria T Bulzacchelli. July 2009. "Effects of state level firearm seller accountability policies on firearm trafficking."

[70] <http://www.ncbi.nlm.nih.gov/pmc/articles/PMC2704273/>. Daniel W Webster, Jon S. Vernick, Maria T Bulzacchelli. July 2009. "Effects of state level firearm seller accountability policies on firearm trafficking."

[71] <http://www.ncbi.nlm.nih.gov/pmc/articles/PMC2704273/>. Daniel W Webster, Jon S. Vernick, Maria T Bulzacchelli. July 2009. "Effects of state level firearm seller accountability policies on firearm trafficking."

[72] <http://www.ncbi.nlm.nih.gov/pmc/articles/PMC2704273/>. Daniel W Webster, Jon S. Vernick, Maria T Bulzacchelli. July 2009. "Effects of state level firearm seller accountability policies on firearm trafficking."

[73] <http://californiaaacep.org/wp-content/uploads/Wintemute-preventing-firearm-violence-what-does-the-research-show-final.pdf>. January 29th, 2013. "Preventing gun violence: what does the research show?" Garen Wintemute, MD, MPH.

[74] <http://content.thirdway.org/publications/11/AGS_Report_-_Selling_Crime_-_High_Crime_Gun_Stores_Fuel_Criminals.pdf> "Selling crime:High crime gun stores fuel criminals." January 2004. Americans for Gun Safety Foundation.

[75] <http://californiaaacep.org/wp-content/uploads/Wintemute-preventing-firearm-violence-what-does-the-research-show-final.pdf>. January 29th, 2013. "Preventing gun violence: what does the research show?" Garen Wintemute, MD, MPH..

[76] From testimony given by Daniel W. Webster of the Johns Hopkins Center for Gun Policy and Research before the Senate Subcommittee on the Constitution, Civil Rights and Human Rights, February 12th, 2013. Paraphrased.

[77] <http://www.justice.gov/oig/reports/ATF/e0406/final.pdf> "Review of the Bureau of Alcohol, Tobacco, Firearms and Explosives Enforcement of Brady Act Violations identified through the National Instant Criminal Backgrouond Check System". Report Number I-2004-006. July 2004. U.S. Department of Justice. Accessed October 14th, 2013.

[1] <http://www.ncbi.nlm.nih.gov/pmc/articles/PMC2759797/> . Charles C Branas, PhD, Therese S Richmond, PhD, CRNP, Dennis P Culhane, PhD, Thomas R Ten Have, PhD, MPH, Douglas J Wiebe, PhD. "Investigating the link between gun possession and gun assault." November 2009.

[2] <http://psycnet.apa.org/journals/xhp/38/5/1159/>. "Wielding a gun increases the bias to see guns." Witt, Jessica K, Brockmole, James R. Journal of Experimental Psychology: Human perception and performance, Vol 38(5), Oct 2012, 1159-1167. doi. 10,1037/a0027881.

[3] <http://www.vpc.org/studies/justifiable.pdf>. August 12th, 2013. Violence Policy Center. "Guns are rarely used to kill criminals or stop crimes new VPC analysis reveals."

[4] <http://www.vpc.org/studies/wmmw2012.pdf> . "When men murder women: An analysis of 2010 homicide data." Violence Policy Center.

[5] <http://www.startribune.com/local/192919031.html>. Brandon Stahl. February 26th, 2013. "BCA stats show self-defense shootings rare for Minnesota permit holders."

[6] <http://www.startribune.com/local/192919031.html>. Brandon Stahl. February 26th, 2013. "BCA stats show self-defense shootings rare for Minnesota permit holders.".

[7] <http://www.csmonitor.com/USA/DC-Decoder/2013/0130/Gun-control-101-Do-Americans-often-use-firearms-in-self-defense>. Peter Grier. January 30, 2013. "Gun Control 101: Do Americans often use firearms in self defense?" Original study in Justice Quarterly. Volume 19, Issue 2, 2002, pp377-398. "An examination of the impact of victim, offender, and situational attributes on the deterrent effect of defensive gun use: A research note."

[8] <http://www.ncbi.nlm.nih.gov/pubmed/15066882>. David Hemenway, Miller M. 2004 Apr; 158(4):395-400.. "Gun threats against and self-defense gun use by California adolescents."

[9] <http://www.ncbi.nlm.nih.gov/pmc/articles/PMC1730664/> . D Hemenway, D Azrael, M Miller. Injury Prevention December 2000. "Gun use in the \United States: results from two national surveys."

[10] Kellerman A., New England Journal of Medicine, 1985.

[11] <http://www.jhsph.edu/research/centers-and-institutes/johns-hopkins-center-for-gun-policy-and-research/publications/IPV_Guns.pdf> . Johns Hopkins Bloomberg School of Public health. "Intimate partner violence and firearms."

[12] <http://www.jhsph.edu/research/centers-and-institutes/johns-hopkins-center-for-gun-policy-and-research/publications/IPV_Guns.pdf>. Johns Hopkins Bloomberg School of Public health. "Intimate partner violence and firearms.".

[13] <http://www.vpc.org/studies/justifiable.pdf>. Violence Policy Center. "Firearm justifiable homicides and non-fatal self-defense gun use."

[14] <http://www.langerresearch.com/uploads/1145a1GunControl.pdf>. "Many see societal issues in CT shootings; Most back ban on high capacity clips." ABC News/Washington Post poll. December 17th, 2012.

[15] <http://en.wikipedia.org/wiki/Sell_your_cloak_and_buy_a_sword> . Last accessed August 15th, 2013.

[16] <http://www.motherjones.com/mojo/2012/12/wayne-lapierre-nra-press-conference-riddled-humiliating-outdated-cultural-references>. Asawin Suebsaeng. December 21st, 2012. "NRA Press conference riddled with weirdly outdated cultural references."

[17] <http://www.nramuseum.org/the-museum/the-galleries/william-b-ruger-special-exhibits.aspx>. Last accessed August 16th, 2013.

[1] <http://www.huffingtonpost.com/2013/04/03/dianne-feinstein-nra_n_3009954.html>. Lisa Heff. April 3rd, 2013. "Dianne Feinstein: NRA intimidation weakens gun control reform."

[2] <http://smartgunlaws.org/wp-content/uploads/2012/05/Banning_Assault_Weapons_A_Legal_Primer_8.05_entire.pdf>. "Banning assault weapons - a legal primer for state and local action.". Legal community against violence. August 2005

[3] <http://thinkprogress.org/gun-debate-guide/> . Zack Beauchamp. January 31st, 2013. "The ultimate guide to the gun safety debate." Original citation: <http://cjchivers.com/post/41366757479/talking-assault-rifles-a-primer-from-the-small>

[4] <http://www.gunpolicy.org/firearms/region/united-states>. Last accessed August 4th, 2013.

[5] <http://www.gunpolicy.org/firearms/region/united-kingdom>. Last accessed August 4th, 2013.

[6] <http://thinkprogress.org/gun-debate-guide/>. Zack Beauchamp. January 31st, 2013.

"The ultimate guide to the gun safety debate."
[7] <http://www.urban.org/UploadedPDF/aw_final.pdf>. "Impact evaluation of the public safety and recreational firearms use protrection act of 1994." The Urban Institute. Jeffrey A. Roth, Christopher S. Koper. March 13, 1997
[8] <http://www.urban.org/UploadedPDF/aw_final.pdf>. "Impact evaluation of the public safety and recreational firearms use protrection act of 1994." The Urban Institute. Jeffrey A. Roth, Christopher S. Koper. March 13, 1997
[9] <https://www.ncjrs.gov/pdffiles1/nij/grants/204431.pdf>. "An updated assessment of the federal assault weapons ban: Impacts on gun markets and gun violence, 1994-2003." Report to the National Institute of Justice, US Department of Justice. Christopher S. Koper, Daniel J. Woods and Jeffrey A. Roth. June 2004.
[10] <http://www.cdc.gov/nchs/data/databriefs/db37.htm> . Arialdi M. Miniño, M.P.H. "Mortality among teenagers aged 12-19 years: United States, 1999-2006." Last accessed August 5th, 2013.
[11] <http://papers.ssrn.com/sol3/papers.cfm?abstract_id=2108854>. Arindrajit Debe, Oeindrila Dube, Omar garcia Ponce. August 13th, 2012. "Cross Border spillover: US. gun laws and violence in Mexico."
[12] <http://www.econ-jobs.com/research/32941-Exporting-the-Second-Amendment-US-Assault-Weapons-and-the-Homicide-Rate-in-Mexico.pdf>. Luke Chicoine, University of Notre Dame. July 18th, 2011. "Exporting the Second Amendment: U.S. assault weapons and the homicide rate in Mexico."
[13] https://www.ncjrs.gov/pdffiles1/nij/grants/204431.pdf . "An updated assessment of the federal assault weapons ban: Impacts on gun markets and gun violence, 1994-2003." Report to the National Institute of Justice, US Department of Justice. Christopher S. Koper, Daniel J. Woods and Jeffrey A. Roth. June 2004.
[14] <http://www.urban.org/UploadedPDF/aw_final.pdf> . "Impact evaluation of the public safety and recreational firearms use protrection act of 1994." The Urban Institute. Jeffrey A. Roth, Christopher S. Koper. March 13, 1997
[15] <https://www.ncjrs.gov/pdffiles1/nij/grants/204431.pdf>. "An updated assessment of the federal assault weapons ban: Impacts on gun markets and gun violence, 1994-2003." Report to the National Institute of Justice, US Department of Justice. Christopher S. Koper, Daniel J. Woods and Jeffrey A. Roth. June 2004.
[16] <https://www.ncjrs.gov/pdffiles1/nij/grants/204431.pdf>. "An updated assessment of the federal assault weapons ban: Impacts on gun markets and gun violence, 1994-2003." Report to the National Institute of Justice, US Department of Justice. Christopher S. Koper, Daniel J. Woods and Jeffrey A. Roth. June 2004..
[17] <https://www.ncjrs.gov/pdffiles1/nij/grants/204431.pdf> . "An updated assessment of the federal assault weapons ban: Impacts on gun markets and gun violence, 1994-2003." Report to the National Institute of Justice, US Department of Justice. Christopher S. Koper, Daniel J. Woods and Jeffrey A. Roth. June 2004..
[18] <https://www.ncjrs.gov/pdffiles1/173405.pdf>. March 1999. Jeffrey A. Roth, Christopher S. Koper. "Impacts of the 1994 Assault Weapons Ban: 1994-96."
[19] <http://www.cnn.com/2012/12/21/us/military-style-weapons-ireport>, Thom Patterson. December 21st, 2012. "Why would someone own a military-style rifle?"
[20] <http://en.wikipedia.org/wiki/Bump_fire>, "Bump Fire". Last Accessed April 5th, 2013.
[21]

<http://militarygunsupply.com/index.php?main_page=product_info&products_id=1082>, Last Accessed April 5th, 2013. Military Gun Supply. "Slide Fire SSAR-15 Bump Fire Stock".

[22] http://www.dailykos.com/story/2013/03/13/1193817/-NRA-defending-felons-from-disarmament# . March 13th, 2013. Tytalus, Daily Kos. "NRA defends felons from disarmament."

[23] <http://www.ar15.com/content/manuals/manual_bushmaster.pdf> , Last Accessed 5th April, 2013.

[24] <http://www.vpc.org/studies/hoseone.htm>. "Ten key points about what assault weapons are and why they are so deadly." Violence Policy Center. Last accessed August 19th, 2013.

[25] <http://www.vpc.org/studies/hoseone.htm>. "Ten key points about what assault weapons are and why they are so deadly." Violence Policy Center. Last accessed August 19th, 2013..

[26] <http://www.policeone.com/officer-shootings/articles/1227784-New-tests-Even-inexperienced-shooters-can-be-fast-accurate-when-shooting-cops/>. "New tests:Even inexperienced shooters can be fast, accurate when shooting cops." March 28th, 2007.

[27] http://www.dailykos.com/story/2012/07/22/1112678/-The-AR-15-your-ideal-home-defense-weapon . Cartoon Peril. July 22nd, 2012. "The AR-15: your ideal home defense weapon?"